Appreciative Living

Appreciative Living

The Principles of Appreciative Inquiry
In Personal Life

Jacqueline Bascobert Kelm

www.AppreciativeLiving.com

Venet
Publishers

To order additional copies or to order in bulk, or for any other questions, please email Admin@AppreciativeLiving.com.

Library of Congress Control Number: 2005931852

Third Edition

ISBN 0-9772161-0-1

Cover design by Jane Pinzauti of La Mamma Design

Venet Publishers
Charleston, SC

www.AppreciativeLiving.com

To All of Us...

Contents

Part II: The Practice

ACKNOWELDGEMENTS

There are many people who have contributed directly to the creation of this book, and many others who supported me in the process. I wrote this while also being a full-time mother of two young children, so you can imagine how long this list will be.

I'll begin at the beginning, with Dawn Cooperrider Dole, the woman who first encouraged me to write. Dawn is one of the great unsung heroines within AI, who works diligently behind the scenes in many capacities to keep AI moving forward. She not only prompted me to create this book, but in doing so helped me discover a passion for writing that might otherwise have lain dormant for years. I can't thank her enough.

Then there is my primary editor, Jane Galloway Seiling, who began working with me at the start and never left my side. She was more than an editor, she was a sponsor and dear friend. She got me back on track during periods of confusion, and encouraged me to stop reading and start writing.

Rita Demarco-Madden is one of my closest friends and mentors, and we deliberated many aspects of this book together. She read every word I wrote and has been such a gift to me in more ways than I can put in writing.

There were many family members and friends who helped out at various stages. My brother Michael Bascobert provided invaluable legal counsel and my brother Paul Bascobert helped with computer and electronic needs. Deanna Danner, Jackie Stavros, Jon Utech, Sue Hammond, Sandra Moncaldo, Kristin Mitchell, and Lisa Davidson read through various parts of my manuscripts, and provided a wealth of diverse suggestions. I also had wonderful conversations with my sisters-in-law Sharon Kelm, Kathy Kelm, Deanna Danner, Jane Kirk, and Julie Jiang, ruminating over a variety of book decisions and considerations.

I also had three "angels" show up at just the right time during this process. I met Heather Therien as I was finishing the first draft, who agreed to read through it during her summer break. She is a brilliant and creative copy editor, who added value to the book well beyond grammar suggestions. I then happened to meet Kate Piersanti over the phone as I was finishing up the final draft, and she generously went through the entire manuscript and provided detailed design, editing, and layout suggestions. Jane Pinzauti came to the rescue one week before I printed the book, and created the most wonderful cover design. I am deeply appreciative of the talent and generosity of all three women, none of whom would accept much beyond a dinner for their incredible effort.

Then there is my personal support system. Jon, my husband of 15 years, could not have been more supportive. He watched our two children almost continuously towards the end, ate a lot more hotdogs for dinner than most, and was my sounding board and major advocate. I love him dearly.

My parents and my husband's parents have always been supportive. My mother and father watched the children for me on occasion, and were always interested in how my writing was going. My father-in-law came to visit during a deadline, and was considerate and understanding while I effectively ignored him the entire weekend.

Finally, there are Cindy Mease and Linda Horn who are amateur photographers. I was hoping to use their inspiring pictures in my book but it did not work out. They were so considerate and understanding through the whole process, and I still hope to find a place for their work.

I am so grateful for each one of you - thank you all.

Be like the bird that,
passing on her flight awhile on boughs too slight,
feels them give way beneath her,
and yet sings,
knowing that she hath wings.

~ VICTOR HUGO

Introduction

The real voyage of discovery consists
not in seeking new landscapes,
but in having new eyes.

~ MARCEL PROUST

Appreciative Inquiry (AI) has transformed my life. My greatest wish and sincere intent in this book is to help others find the sheer joy in living that is available to all of us. AI has traditionally been used to transform organizations, but it is equally transformative in individuals. There are many who say that in order to "do it" in organizations, you have to "be it" in your personal life. This is a book about "being it."

This book was written both for people who are familiar with AI in organizations, as well as those who are new to the concept. If you apply AI in organizations, living these principles will make you more effective in your organizational work as you "walk the talk." If you are new to AI, you may experience a fundamental paradigm shift as you come to understand how you are creating the life you experience. You will also learn practical ways to shift your thinking and actions to create more joy and happiness than you ever thought possible.

In the pages ahead we will journey into the conscious and unconscious domains of our minds as we explore how we think and what we say. I'll explain how we create our personal identity and reality with others, and consider the tremendous implications of that concept. We'll explore the nature of our underlying beliefs and assumptions and how they influence our present and future. I'll discuss the rationale for shifting our thinking habits to notice the good and to appreciate the best in ourselves and each moment. We'll look at the continuous nature of change and the power of questions and small steps to direct those changes. Finally, we'll consider the impact of our images and beliefs about the future and learn ways to deliberately create what we want most.

How To Read This Book

Prepare your mind to receive the best that life has to offer. ~Ernest Holmes

I wrote this book with two different kinds of people in mind: people like me who love to analyze things, and people like my dear friend Sandra who do not. Part I of this book, "The Philosophy," is for people like me. It is full of the latest theory and research about AI across multiple disciplines, and goes into depth on the original and emergent principles. It explains why the AI principles make sense and how they work. I could just eat these chapters up.

Part II, "The Practice," is for Sandra. She took a look at one of my favorite chapters and basically said, "Is anybody really going to read all this stuff?" I picked my ego up off the floor, and created Part II. Chapter 7 contains a simple three-step process we can use in our daily affairs to apply the AI principles. Chapter 8 includes exercises we can do to help shift our automatic thinking. The exercises are simple, and most can be done in 15 minutes or less.

Chapter 9 is "Nirvana" for the "Sandras" of the world. It contains bullet point summaries of all the ideas in the book and is a nice reference guide.

If you want to really understand the principles, then I suggest you read and savor Part I before going on to Part II. If

you don't care to read through all the theory, then you might
want to simply skip to Part II, "The Practice." If you have
questions about any particular area, you can always go back
into the earlier chapters to learn more. Either way, enjoy!

What is Appreciative Inquiry?

*The optimist proclaims that we live in the best of all
possible worlds; and the pessimist fears
this is true. ~James Branch Cabell*

AI was first conceptualized at Case Western Reserve
University in 1980 by doctoral student David Cooperrider and
his thesis advisor, Suresh Srivastva.[1] Jane Watkins and Bernard
Mohr provide a beautifully detailed history of the beginnings
of AI in their book, *Appreciative Inquiry: Change at the Speed
of Imagination*.[2] They describe the detailed events of how AI
began as a theory-building process and eventually evolved into
the change philosophy it has become today.

Fundamentally, "AI is about the co-evolutionary search for
the best in people, their organizations, and the relevant world
around them."[3] It is a positive, strength-based approach to
change. It includes co-creating inspiring images of what we
want, and then building on positive aspects to make them
happen. It means becoming more aware of our internal and
external dialogues and intentionally shifting them to focus on
what we want more of. It unleashes the positive potential
within people and situations through attention and focus on the
positive core. It suggests we build on our strengths, successes,
and best practices to achieve our greatest hopes and dreams. AI
is all this and more.

AI is a "living," "organic" concept that continuously
emerges and grows with new learning and information. This
book contains new thinking from various disciplines that is
consistent with the principles of AI and adds to the evolving

repertoire of beliefs. Appreciative Living is simply applying Appreciative Inquiry in everyday life. For additional information on Appreciative Inquiry visit the Case Western Reserve University AI website at www.appreciativeinquiry.case.edu or my website at www.AppreciativeLiving.com.

The Principles of AI

We can easily forgive a child who is afraid of the dark. The real tragedy of life is when men are afraid of the light. ~Plato

In the early 1990's, David Cooperrider created the five original principles[4] of AI under the guidance of Suresh Srivastva, which describe the basic tenets of the underlying philosophy. The five principles are: the Constructionist Principle, the Poetic Principle, the Simultaneity Principle, the Anticipatory Principle, and the Positive Principle. A summary of all the principles can be found in Chapter 9.

AI consultants have recently started adding to the principles to reflect new learning and thinking. In 2003 Diana Whitney and Amanda Trosten-Bloom proposed three additional principles in their book *The Power of Appreciative Inquiry*. They are: The Wholeness Principle, the Enactment Principle, and the Free Choice Principle.[5] These principles were created out of the authors' experience with large-scale organizations and community change work in an effort to further define the ever-emerging concept of AI. In addition, Frank Barrett and Ron Fry are proposing the Narrative Principle in their book *Appreciative Inquiry: A Positive Approach to Cooperative Capacity Building.*[6] Finally, Jackie Stavros and Cheri Torres recommended the Awareness Principle in their book *Dynamic Relationships: Unleashing the Power of Appreciative Inquiry in Daily Living.*[7]

Each chapter in this book contains the relevant theory and practices that have emerged around the original and emergent principles from different disciplines. These disciplines include social construction, positive psychology, strength-based therapy, chaos theory, self-organizing systems, biology, quantum mechanics, and others. The concepts in these chapters are by no means all-inclusive. As I now write I sit with a shelf full of unread books, bulging with ideas that would add to this discussion. There came a time when I had to freeze my thoughts and understandings and write it all down.

The important thing to remember is that Appreciative Living is a journey and not a destination. It requires deliberate effort over time to shift our automatic thinking and open our minds and hearts. These pages present a pioneering look at the AI principles, and a few of the myriad of ways to incorporate them into our personal lives.

Part I

The Philosophy

CHAPTER 1

The Constructionist Principle

We don't live in a world of reality, we live in a world of perceptions.

~ GERARD J. SIMMONS

The Constructionist Principle conceptually underlies the other principles in Appreciative Inquiry (AI.) The essential premise is that life experience doesn't just happen to us, we actually create it together. This concept is quite deep and fairly abstract, but it has profound implications for how we participate in life. This chapter is one of the most difficult to get through, but offers some of the most valuable insights in how we create our lives. David Cooperrider first wrote about this principle with consulting partner Diana Whitney:

> Simply stated—human knowledge and organizational destiny are interwoven…we must be adept in the art of understanding, reading, and analyzing organizations as living, human constructions. Knowing stands at the center of any and virtually every attempt at change. Thus, the way we know is fateful.[1]

Cooperrider and Whitney are addressing organizations, but each of us is, in effect, an organization. We construct our understandings of who we and others are, and these constructions become our reality.

Within the Constructionist Principle, Diana Whitney and Amanda Trosten-Bloom say that "meaning is made in conversation, reality is created in communication, and knowledge is generated through social interaction. These exchanges can be verbal or non-verbal, and they add that language is the vehicle through which we create our understanding of the world. Harlene Anderson expands on this last point:

> We are in continuous conversation with each other and with ourselves. Through conversation we form and reform our life experiences and events; we create and recreate our meanings and understandings; and we construct and reconstruct our realities and our selves. Some conversations enhance possibility; others diminish it.[2]

Social constructionism suggests there is no true reality "out there." We are each creating our own version of "what's really going on," and no two people see it exactly the same way. We each live in the worlds we have created, which include our beliefs about who we are.

Although we are creating our own individual experience of reality, we are deeply influenced by others in our constructions. The next section describes the nature of this influence, which is so pervasive we are often not aware of the extent to which others shape our beliefs and experience.

Reality is Co-Created

*I have learned silence from the talkative, toleration
from the intolerant, and kindness from the
unkind; yet strange, I am ungrateful
to those teachers. ─Kahlil Gibran*

We come to understand the world as we engage with other
people, ourselves, cultures, animals, nature, a higher power etc.
Reality is basically our experience of what is going on in any
given moment, and our self-image is part of that reality. Who
we are and what we believe about things are not fixed notions,
but are continuously re-created in conversations and
communications with others. We are *linguistically constructed,
relational selves.*[3] Let's consider a practical example of how
this works.

Example of Co-Creation

Susan grew up in a middle class suburban culture, where
responsibility was a valued trait that had been passed down
through many generations. Her parents talked to her about
responsibility, told stories of others who acted accordingly or
not, and rewarded her for acting responsibly. They shaped her
understanding of responsibility as following through on what
she promised and doing what was expected. Susan's
understanding was sharpened and reinforced in school and later
in the workplace with good reports, awards, and recognition for
responsible behavior. She observed mother animals responsibly
caring for their young, and honed her understanding further.
Her religious organization taught that responsibility was good
and would be rewarded in the end. The media emphasized the
importance of being consistent with the prevailing norms and
expectations of society, which added further to her
construction.

Susan has come to *believe* that responsibility is a good trait and one that she possesses. Her understanding is unique, since no one else comes at it with the exact same set of experiences and conversations that she does. Others will view responsibility differently based on their particular influences.

As Susan talks with a friend about responsibility, they *co-create* or *co-construct* understanding together through language. Each girl influences the other, and the meaning they create together is sometimes said to exist in the "conversational space" between the two of them.[4] The following story of Susan as a teenager illustrates the idea of co-construction:

> Susan sees her new friend Shawna running towards her in the hall at school. She gets that uneasy feeling inside as Shawna approaches. "Hey Susan," Shawna exclaims, "let's get out of here and go to the park for a few hours. Mr. Davidson will never miss us!" Susan can feel her head swimming. The voices of her mother, teachers, family, friends, religion, and culture instantly race through her mind with opinions about what she should do. She looks at the ground, and says, "I don't know about just leaving like that." Shawna jumps in, "What's wrong with just having a little fun?" Susan shifts uneasily and begins to wonder about all the fun she misses out on by following the rules. She looks at her beliefs about responsibility from a new perspective and replies, "How about if we stop at the cafeteria and get a drink before the next class instead?" As innocent as this may sound, it is a radical thing for Susan to do. Shawna pauses and reflects on the realization that her new friend is one of those people who always follows the rules. She considers what it would be like to live that way for a moment, and shifts her beliefs slightly about the value of responsibility. She rolls her eyes and sighs, "Well, okay."

Each girl will walk away from the interaction with newly co-constructed notions of responsibility, how important it is, and how it fits into her personal identity. The shift might be slight, but both will have gained new understanding through this interaction that will be melded in with previous beliefs and experiences.

The Collective Person

Susan from the previous example has come to believe that responsibility is a good trait and one that she possesses. This understanding was created within the context of all her relationships. Although Susan experiences it as her own individual belief, it is actually a *collective* or *co-created* belief, in that it is a product of many different interactions. Susan develops her self image from the culmination of all her co-constructed beliefs. She develops her beliefs about others in the same manner.

Jane Galloway Seiling uses the term "collective person" to represent the notion that each of us is a collective product of all our interactions. She uses the metaphor of the formation of the Mississippi River to describe the formation of the self.[5] She explains how the river begins with droplets from the originating streams and tributaries, and grows with additions from other small and large rivers, fields, and streams. She describes how the droplets all merge together to form the river, and it would be difficult to determine the influences or origins of any one drop. She concludes that each person is like the Mississippi: a collective notion formed and altered through the contacts, experiences, learnings, desires, and actions of multiple others.

The collective person suggests that all we know and believe about ourselves and others is a subjective opinion based on the views and conventions of the families and schools and societies in which we live. These beliefs continuously change as we engage with new people and experiences, and we are never the same person from one moment to the next. We are viewed differently by each individual, and our self-concept is simultaneously molded and reformed by that very person. It is through the eyes of others that we come to know ourselves and all that we experience.

Our collective self makes sense within the communities and cultures in which we live. If Susan were suddenly transported to an inner city gang culture her notion of responsibility would change dramatically. Her beliefs and behaviors would be viewed as foreign by this new group, and what she has come to believe about herself and reality would be challenged.

Strong beliefs we have about our collective self and reality can eventually become truths. A truth is simply a belief we have come to accept as true to a stronger degree than other beliefs. It is the relationships around us that keep our beliefs and truths relevant and intact.

Truth is Local

Our own life is the instrument with which we experiment with truth[6]. ~Thich Nhat Hanh

Because social constructionism suggests there is no absolute truth or objective reality,[7] we all create our sense about "what's really going on" in a way that is unique to us. Our understanding is not the "truth" about what is happening, it is only our version of it. Others will experience the same situation differently and come to different conclusions about "what's going on." I saw a bumper sticker once that aptly proclaimed, "Don't believe everything you think."

Truth is a Construction

Life is not experienced in a vacuum. We simultaneously integrate our past and present beliefs as we construct a new reality with others. As we hear over and over from different sources that being responsible is a good way to live, we begin to view that as "truth." We come to believe that it is better to follow the rules, do what we promise, and adhere to the standards and norms of our society. We carry that truth into our next experience and act accordingly. It is only "truth" for us, from our relative perspective and framework of understanding. It will be viewed differently by others. For example, Hippies of the 1960's considered it irresponsible to embrace the status quo; they responsibly rebelled against the norms of society.

Our constructions are continuously changing and are only "true" in this moment. In the next moment, as Susan from our previous example experiences a mid-life crisis, she may view her years of responsibility as a restraining noose that prevented her from living the life she really wanted to live. One significant event, such as winning the lottery, can shift a lifetime of beliefs about what we thought was true.

So, is responsibility a good trait? It depends on who you ask. The responsible, conscientious mother would answer "yes." The defiant, rebellious teenager would respond "no." Again, who is right? Social constructionists would say the question of who is right, or whose perspective is more valid, is not of issue. No two people will see it the same way, and one person's truth or reality is no more true than another's. Let's suppose we were to call in a "neutral" third party to determine the "real" truth. Again, his assessment will be a construction created within his unique framework of understanding, values, and life experiences. He might be seen as neutral to some, and biased to others.

What if the third party is an "expert" in psychology and moral philosophy? Now we are placing a value judgment on the quality of the construction. We are saying some people are more qualified to create the truth than others. We do this every day and it serves an important function in making our world work. And yet, in the social constructionist's view, the expert opinion is no more true in the absolute sense than anyone else's opinion.

Local Truth

Social constructionists are not suggesting we abandon the search for truth as such, but instead that we recognize there is no ultimate truth or meaning that supersedes all others. There is tremendous value in creating what Kenneth and Mary Gergen call "local truth,"[8] an agreement about what is true within a community of people. This is fundamentally how we exist. The truths that are created within communities have meaning and value within those communities, but not necessarily beyond. Beliefs about what is true are specific to these groups of people, and others outside the community may not see it the same way. Gergen and Gergen describe this idea further:

> The idea of truth within community is of enormous consequence…it is important within a community of rocket scientists to know whether it is true or false that a rocket will follow a certain trajectory; this truth is wedded to the value they place on safely reaching a destination…Our troubles begin, however, when local claims to truth (t) are treated as transcendental truth (T), when one community claims that the world was created by a Big Bang and another by a Big God, when one claims that homosexuality is a disorder and another that it is a normal human activity, or one claims that all behavior is determined and another that people have free will. Like most claims to knowledge, the humility of the local is replaced by the arrogance of the universal.[9]

Authorities on Truth

There are some who contend that scientific truth is the ultimate truth. "Data doesn't lie," is a common phrase in these communities yet there is always a person who must interpret the data and assign a meaning to it or significance of some sort. Subjective decisions are made about what data to collect, how to collect it, and what it ultimately means. Conclusions are determined from the data about what is relevant, true, important, and possible. As new scientific discoveries are made, the truth, beliefs, and possibilities expand. People previously believed the sun revolved around the Earth until Galileo proved otherwise. Quantum mechanics demonstrated the limits of Newtonian physics. Scientific facts and theories are discovered and become obsolete along with our personal beliefs.

There is one other common alleged authority on what is right and true: religious or spiritual authority. This is tenuous territory upon which to tread, and possibly the most sensitive. If the higher power of any religion, be it God, Buddha, Allah, or some other deity, bestows the "real" truth, then consider how we gain access to that truth. Some find it in passages from their chosen sacred texts, or from the teachings of religious and spiritual authorities. Others say they speak directly to God, angels, spiritual masters, or other entities. Regardless of the process or source from which we get the information, we must still interpret it and construct the meaning of it, through the lens of our personal values and beliefs. Two people studying the same Biblical passage may come away with different beliefs about the meaning of that passage. Even in matters of faith, we individually and uniquely construct our truth. Once again, it is not about whose truth is *most* true, but about recognizing the personal and local nature of our individual truths.

Let us be clear that social constructionism is not saying there is or is not a God; that is up to each of us and what we choose to construct. I have very strong personal beliefs about God, but that is my local truth. It is based on my co-constructed beliefs in the same way an atheist proclaims there is no God. Some think a woman's right to choose abortion is a bad thing, others think it is a good thing. Some think conformity is desirable while others do not. The truth depends on the beliefs within the community of people whom you are asking.

Our spiritual beliefs are some of the most deep and pervasive beliefs we hold. The miracle of life on earth, the purpose of our existence, the mysteries of life after death; our spiritual beliefs address these questions and many others. They drive most of our daily decisions and actions, either directly or indirectly. Suggesting that such powerful beliefs may not be "true" in the absolute sense can be very unsettling, and even offensive.

This discussion begs the question, "Are we basically making it all up?" Well, yes we are, in a sense. We're making it all up together. The point is not to lament the idea that there are no foundations for absolute truth, but to acknowledge that the foundation of truth and belief on which we base our lives, is our own co-creation. It can be as small as a married couple believing in monogamy, or as big as the whole world believing that the earth is round.

In summary, our local truths or common beliefs help us function and organize our personal experience. They provide tremendous value and importance in our affairs, but they are not absolute, and they are ours alone as a collective person. This idea can be disconcerting at first, but ultimately it is empowering as we realize that we are much more free than we ever imagined to construct truth in a way that ultimately serves us well.

We See Things As We Are

*We do not see things as they are, we see them
as we are. ~Anais Nin*

We construct reality in relationships with others through the
lenses of our beliefs, assumptions, traditions, and norms. We
come into a situation with a lifetime of co-constructed filters
that influence what we perceive in the moment. In this sense,
we see things as we are, and not in some objective sense. We
can expand our beliefs by opening up to the ways that others
view a situation. The more different a person is from us, the
greater the learning and growth potential.

   We are never truly neutral observers. For example, if a
young boy were to come upon a homeless man for the first
time asleep in the street, the boy might determine that he is a
camper who has lost his tent and is very fortunate in not having
to take a bath. This conclusion would fit with the boy's current
beliefs and previous experiences of camping and bathing that
he has determined as relevant.

   If the same boy comes upon the homeless man with his
mother, his construction will be influenced by her beliefs. If
she is a homeless shelter volunteer, the explanation she gives
about the man and what he is doing would probably be
supportive and empathetic of his situation. If the mother is a
disgruntled business owner who is losing customers because of
the homeless disturbance, the description of the man and his
choices would probably be a lot different. In each case she is
viewing the situation through the lenses of her previous
understandings and will influence the boy's construction
accordingly. As the boy questions his mother about why the
homeless person lives as he does, there is an opportunity for
the mother to reflect on her underlying assumptions, and
expand the filter of her beliefs. The mother's and boy's
individual understandings of homelessness will be co-created

through their interaction as they talk about the homeless situation together.

Our underlying beliefs and assumptions play an important role in our normal functioning. They sometimes appear as liabilities in our discussions, but they provide us the opportunity to make sense of our world in an efficient way. They speed up our ability to make decisions and take action. We would be overwhelmed without them, given everything we have to process in a single moment. The suggestion in social construction is to take time when appropriate to question our underlying thinking, thereby growing in understanding. The concern is that we can go through life on "auto-pilot," automatically accepting and allowing our co-constructed beliefs and assumptions to guide us through situations. This limits our ability to learn and grow with experience, since we tend to repeat the same things over and over.

When you begin to look at all the things you consider to be true through the lens of social construction, you realize that there are a lot of assumptions you have automatically accepted rather than intentionally and thoughtfully integrated. Does everyone want a lot of money? Have aliens visited the Earth? Do bad people go to Hell? Questioning our underlying assumptions allows us to expand our thinking.

Children provide a wonderful opportunity to surface assumptions and expand beliefs. Their relatively open filters lead to unique questions and comments that often stimulate interesting new insights. I have given pause numerous times to reflect on questions from my children such as: "Where does dirt come from?"..."Are you going to die before me?"..."Why do I have to wear clothes?"..."Are trees made of wood?"

I remember one particular family conversation that reminded me about local truth. My 4-year old son was explaining that he wanted to be a fire fighter and a spaceman when he grew up. My husband said those sounded like good choices, since he would be able to do exciting things. My son replied in an indignant voice, "No Dad, it's because they all wear boots."

We become much less concerned about getting others to see it "our way" when we understand that we each experience a different reality. I could have tried to convince my son that traveling into space is more exciting than wearing boots, but in doing so I would be missing the opportunity to learn from his perspective. After all, maybe he's "right."

When we allow others in the conversation to have their beliefs without resistance, an interesting thing begins to happen: *we now have more time in the exchange for listening*. We begin to realize that the way we grow and learn is by listening to how others view a situation and the meaning they develop. We find that the more different a person is from us, the more it causes us to reflect on our taken-for-granted thoughts, and the more we can learn. As we attempt to understand the unique way another makes sense, we open ourselves to new horizons of thinking and understanding. This is the value of diversity and the spirit of true inquiry.

We discover it is often valuable to try to see things another's way and then fit that into our understanding. Author and coach Stephen Covey writes that the "Fifth habit of highly effective people" is "Seek first to understand, then to be understood."[10] We also find that other people become a lot more interesting as we let go of our need to be right, and attempt to discover more about them. Gay Hendricks describes it this way:

> ...the central choice of conscious living [is] whether
> to open ourselves in wonder to what needs to be
> learned or felt or resolved, or to contract into
> opinion, belief, and justification...every utterance
> out of our mouths serves one of two intentions:
> discovery or justification.[11]

When we listen to others with the sincere desire to see it their way, a win-win situation occurs. We gain insight into our own underlying beliefs and truths, and our partners receive one of the greatest gifts another can bestow: to be heard.

When we accept the idea that we see things as we are, we can let go of our quest for who and what is "right" in the absolute sense. This opens us to new ways of knowing and offers opportunities for learning and growth. The more different people and experiences are, the greater the opportunity for learning, if we are open to it.

We Are Deeply Inter-Connected

We are each made and imagined in the eyes of one another. ~David Cooperrider

It becomes apparent that we are deeply inter-connected when we consider the concepts of the Constructionist Principle. We are continually influencing and being influenced as we construct our reality. Our connections run deeper than we may be aware.

The Influences of Others

There are several bodies of research depicting our interrelatedness with others. The "Pygmalion effect" is one of the most well-known, as a special case of the "self-fulfilling prophecy" concept from psychologist Robert Merton's work.[12] "Pygmalion" was the original name of the George Bernard Shaw play *My Fair Lady,* which popularized the concept.[13] In the classic Pygmalion study,[14] teachers are told that their students have either high, average, or low potential. What the teachers do not know is that these assignments are random. Over time, the high potential students clearly emerge above the others, based solely on the expectations of the teacher. Literally hundreds of studies over the past twenty years have confirmed these results. Cooperrider explains that, "significant Pygmalion effects have been experimentally generated in as little time as fifteen minutes and have the apparent capacity to transform the course of a lifetime."[15]

Aspects of the placebo studies further confirm the Pygmalion effect. These studies show that some people get better with "sugar pills" simply from their belief that the pills will work. What has also been documented is that the effects are strongest when the treating physician also believes in the effectiveness of the placebo.[16] Again this shows that the images projected onto us by others have quite an effect.

As discussed before, our identity is continuously molded and shaped by the influences of others. Consultant and author Margaret Wheatley explains that, "Each organism maintains a clear sense of its individual identity within a larger network of relationships that helps shape its identity. Each being is noticeable as a separate entity, yet it is simultaneously part of the whole system."[17] We influence the collective whole through our projected images, and the collective whole projects back on us.

The Greater Collective

There is an even more pervasive type of connection that has been suggested by some. Physicist David Bohm describes it as the *implicate order*,[18] biologist Rupert Sheldrake as the *morphogenetic field*,[19] and psychologist Carl Jung as the *collective unconscious*.[20] Wheatley summarizes Sheldrake's concept of morphic fields:

> Morphic fields are built up through the skills that accumulate as members of the same species learn something new. After some number (not specified) of a species have learned a behavior, such as bicycle riding, others of that same species will be able to

learn that skill more easily. The behavior collects in
the morphic field, and when an individual's energy
combines with it, the field patterns the behavior of
that individual. They don't have to actually learn the
skill; they pull it from the field.[21]

The essential proposition is that we are influencing and being
influenced by a larger invisible, intangible field. Some also
suggest that it's not just humans and animals that participate in
this larger collective. Random number generators have also
shown erratic behavior in response to life events.

Senge et al explain how random number generators acted
in non-random ways during the US terrorist attacks on
September 11, 2001. The abnormal behavior matched the
chronology of the terrorist attacks, beginning at 5am EST,
peaking at 11am, and staying deviant into the evening.[22] A
report in the *Foundations of Physics Letters* stated in response
that, "we are obliged to confront the possibility that the
measured correlations may be directly associated with some (as
yet poorly understood) aspect of consciousness attendant to
global events."[23]

One other controversial and exploratory area of study is
the freezing water research conducted by Masaru Emoto of
Japan. Emoto subjects water to a variety of conditions, and
then takes pictures of the crystals that form when it freezes.
Senge summarizes the results of Emoto's work in *Presence*:[24]
He describes how water taken from polluted urban sources
forms only partial structures, but water from especially pure or
healthy sources such as springs and deep wells, forms
stunningly complex and beautiful structures.

The same results were obtained by writing certain words
on the outside of vials of distilled water. "For example, the
word 'beautiful' in Japanese (or other languages) produces
exquisite lacy crystals, while the word 'dirty' produces
undeveloped crystals that you could only call ugly."[25] In

another experiment he showed the power of prayer to change the crystal structure. Senge explains:

> ...in one experiment they took water from a highly polluted river reservoir and froze it. The samples had virtually no crystal structure. Then an elder priest, Reverend Kato, sat next to the reservoir and prayed for one hour for the well-being of the water. When they then took new samples of the water and froze it, the crystals were stunning...[26]

Senge also states that the crystals from water that were exposed to music seemed to reflect the music: "the geometric precision of Bach, the balance of order and flow of Mozart, the beautiful simplicity of folk music." Emoto's initial interest in this work stemmed from the fact that our adult bodies are about 75% water by weight.

Our Inter-Relatedness

There is no denying our interdependency with others whether you agree with these theories or not. As Wheatley explains, "None of us exists independent of our relationships with others. Different settings and people evoke some qualities from us and leave others dormant. In each of these relationships, we are different, new in some way."[27] Stavros and Torres describe our inter-relatedness in their book, *Dynamic Relationships:*

> We are relational beings, integrally connected to one another and our environment. Our relationships deeply inform who we are and how we act, which in turn impact others at "this moment"—impacting the "next instant" in the relationship. Our actions and their impact on others are inseparable. We are interconnected.[28]

We are just beginning to explore the extent of our inter-connectedness with others in the west (though some cultures and religions have long held these views). We exist within a web of relationships that provide influence and meaning beyond what's readily apparent. We realize that what we do to others ultimately affects us as well. It starts to become more about us and less about me as we shift from a sense of isolation to one of connection. There are many who think our survival depends on it.

Words Create Worlds

In language we build our own identities, our relationships with others, the countries that we live in, the companies we have, and the values that we hold dear. With language we generate life. ~Fernando Flores

"Words create worlds" is a common phrase in AI that captures the importance of language in our constructions. Narrative therapists Michael White and David Epston say that the reality we create and our self understanding is mediated through language.[29] The words we use to communicate with others profoundly affect the meaning generated between us.

The Meaning of Words

The constructions that we make of reality are primarily created through conversations, yet Ken Gergen describes how language is inadequate to fully convey meaning. There are many factors to consider in language, such as the words we choose, context, patterns of exchange, shared meanings, and so on.[30] For example, there are some words such as "sadness" or "love" which encompass such a broad range of meaning, it is not possible to capture the essence in just one word. Entire poems are written to capture the fullness of a word such as love, yet no two poems are the same.

When we use a word such as love in a conversation, we have no way of knowing how it is being received. The other person may be totally misinterpreting our statement because he or she has a different understanding of the word we are using. Other forms of communication such as writing, pictures, and art are inexact for conveying meaning for the same reasons. The point is not to give up on trying to communicate, but to acknowledge that our ability to share meaning is limited with language and the meanings we individually attribute.

As much as words have limitation in their ability to convey meaning, our choice of words is very influential in the meaning that gets created. Organizational theorist Karl Weick describes how vivid words draw attention to new possibilities.[31] He gives the example of how changing terminology from "intentional ill treatment" to "battered-child" was an important factor in mobilizing action for abused children. The realization of the power of words to convey meaning has caused other language shifts, such as moving from "handicapped" to "physically challenged" and from "black" to "African American."

Metaphor

Metaphor is another interesting language scheme. A metaphor is basically a word or idea that is used to represent a similar concept. For example, the metaphor of a growing plant might be used to represent a new, emerging business. When we combine the constructionist concept of truth to metaphor, an interesting proposition emerges. If there is no real truth about things, then is a metaphor any less true than the thing it represents?

Gergen gives the example of using the metaphor of war to describe an argument.[32] If we begin to think in terms of this metaphor, then our experience of an argument itself can become war-like. The next time we get into a disagreement, we may think in terms of war, and our personal experience will follow. If we change the metaphor for argument, as Gergen suggests, to something such as dance, then our experience of an argument can take on dance-like qualities. The next time we disagree with someone, we may think in terms of moving or flowing with them, perhaps with the intensity of a Tango.

Metaphor is not just a helpful way to describe something, it actually creates the thing it describes. This is the concept of words creating worlds. Metaphors are powerful tools because they distance us from the concept, which breaks down our defenses. It is easier to look at and analyze something "out there" rather than in our selves or our organizations. We can look at areas of our lives that we want to improve and create metaphors that represent them. We can then study the metaphor in a less threatening way and translate the insights into our personal life.

For example, if we continue with the dance metaphor we could also apply it to a relationship with a significant other. We could study in what ways our relationship is like a dance; what it means to lead and follow, dance together and apart, dance the same dance, and so on. As we study the nature of dancing together we might become aware of insights that were too "charged" for us to see without the separation of the metaphor.

Other Linguistic Considerations

The use of metaphor and other linguistic methods to affect change is applied extensively in therapy. Solution-focused therapists O'Hanlon and Weiner-Davis believe that "the creative and mindful use of language is the single most influential indirect method for creating contexts in which change is perceived to be inevitable."[33] The language changes they use are subtle, but powerful.

The first use of language they describe is verb tense. For example, when talking about a problem with a client, they describe it in past-tense. Instead of saying, "you have problem

X," they would say something like, "you've had problem X for a while now."[34] When I first read this, I honestly thought it was too trivial to be of use. Over time I have come to see the value, but it is not necessarily obvious at first glance. The change is subtle, but it opens the door for a new possibility going forward. Instead of talking about our problems as things we have, we can talk about them as things we have had until now.

A second way O'Hanlon and Weiner-Davis describe the mindful use of language is in what they call *possibility* terms versus *definitive* terms.[35] Instead of asking a client, "What *will* you do when problem X occurs?" they ask something like, "What *might* you do?" Again, the language shift is minor, but it loosens the hold on the fixed nature of problem responses and suggests that next time it might be different.

There is one final subtle language trend that I've observed across various disciplines. It is the use of verbs in place of nouns to capture the fluid, ever-changing nature of our selves and our reality. For example, Wheatley and Kellner-Rogers suggest it is more helpful to think of "organizing" rather than "organizations" to convey the continuous creation of structures, processes, and patterns of behavior that define them.[36] Jane Galloway Seiling proposes decisioning as an ongoing process in organizations rather than decision-making as discreet actions.[37] Personal consultants Walter and Peller like the term "preferencing" in therapy work rather than "goal," to convey the non-linear complexities and spontaneity of human events.[38] They also prefer "storying" rather than "stories" to reduce the notion of stories as a fixed, bounded concept that needs to be changed. (We'll talk about stories in the Narrative Principle.)

Harlene Anderson mentions the term "one's selves" in place of oneself. This better represents the collective nature of opinion that we have come to think of as our self. Another variation of this concept is using "human being" instead of "person." This term implies the moment-to-moment nature of our humanness, where we are "being" who we are in one moment, and "being" something different in the next. Terms like appreciative organizing, appreciative living, and appreciative leading, also convey more fluid and dynamic notions than appreciative organizations, appreciative life, or appreciative leadership. I'm not proposing name changes, but simply pointing out how words affect our images and understandings in ways that can be subtle.

In summary, the theory and practice around language usage is extensive, and we've only touched the surface here. The main idea is that our choice of words not only describes our reality, but it creates it as well. Language is the medium through which we create meaning with others, and it has inherent limitations as well as opportunities. The more we understand this concept, the more deliberate we can be in selecting words that create more of what we want.

Final Thoughts

The Constructionist Principle is one of the deepest and most fundamental principles within AI. It suggests that reality is socially created, and there are as many versions of it as there are people. Our identity is part of our reality, and is an ever-emerging, collective product of opinions that we have accepted. There is no absolute truth about ourselves or anything else, but local truths are vitally important in helping us live and make sense of our world. We continuously co-construct reality through the lens of our simultaneously changing beliefs and assumptions, and language is the vehicle through which we describe and create our lives.

These ideas can be a lot to swallow. We are essentially saying that life experience does not happen to us: we continuously co-create it through our myriad of seemingly insignificant daily conversations. The good news about this idea is that we can let go of fixed notions of who we are and what we are living. The ability to create our ideal life is as close as our next conversation.

CHAPTER 2

The Poetic Principle

*The moment one gives close attention to
anything, even a blade of grass, it becomes
a mysterious, awesome, indescribably
magnificent world in itself.*

~ HENRY MILLER

The Poetic Principle suggests that "pasts, presents, or futures
are endless sources of learning, inspiration, or interpretation—
precisely like, for example, the endless interpretive possibilities
in a good piece of poetry or a biblical text."[1] We can find
whatever we want in a person or situation: good and bad, right
and wrong, beautiful and ugly. What we choose to focus on
creates our reality. The more attention we give to something,
the more it expands as part of our experience.

Life Experience is Rich

Reality leaves a lot to the imagination.
~John Lennon

The Poetic Principle suggests that no matter what we want to
find in a situation, organization, or person, it is in there
somewhere. Narrative therapists talk about the idea of lived
experience being "rich."[2] There are a limitless number of

things we can notice in any moment, and our choice is fateful. It is the classic example of one thousand people witnessing an accident and finding one thousand different accounts of what happened. Each person is paying attention to something different—and they see it through their own lens of reality.

Appreciative Inquiry (AI) assumes that each person and "living system has many untapped and rich and inspiring accounts of the positive."[3] For example, some people look at poor, starving people from third world countries and see hopelessness, poverty, and destitution. Mother Teresa, on the other hand, saw God in these people.[4] She was able to do more for them by seeing their strength and beauty than in focusing on the hopelessness of their situation.

When I walk into my workplace there are an infinite number of things on which I can focus my attention. I can notice characteristics of the room such as style, cleanliness, orderliness, and spaciousness. I can pay attention to the people and notice their appearance, actions, and expressions. I can focus on myself and reflect on my appearance, thoughts, and feelings. Every moment is full of things to pay attention to and what we choose to notice creates our experience.

When we come from a traditional belief that reality is something we observe rather than create, it can be hard to accept that we can find anything we want in a person or our self. There is always more present in the collective image of who we are that is endearing, positive and hopeful. It is sometimes more difficult to see these things in ourselves or others depending on how deeply we hold to our current beliefs. As we focus on the positive aspects we help bring them to life and shift our beliefs accordingly. We are rich in positive potential.

We have to realize again from the Constructionist Principle chapter, that our truth about reality is local, and not the only way to see it. There are an infinite number of things we can pay attention to in a given situation or individual, and our choice is fateful.

We Have Habits of Seeing

It's not "seeing is believing;" it's "believing
is seeing." ~The Santa Clause II

We tend to notice the same things over and over in given situations. We have certain "habits" about how we look at what is happening. Senge, Scharmer, Jaworski, and Flowers explain:

> With just the slightest pause, we can begin to
> appreciate the symphony of activities and
> experiences, past and present, that come
> together in each simple moment of awareness.
> Yet out of the symphony we typically hear only
> one or two notes. And these, almost always, are
> the ones most familiar to us.[5]

Our choice about what to pay attention to is a relational decision that is a function of many factors. It includes the implicit questions we ask, such as, "what's important to pay attention to here, what's relevant, or what's interesting to me?" These implicit questions are driven by such things as our collective beliefs, stories, norms, and assumptions. Our focus is also a function of the others present in the moment and our relationships with them. We are influenced by the people with us who call our attention to certain aspects of a situation. We are also influenced by other "voices" in our heads from past experiences. These might be a supportive teacher's voice as we decide to write a book, or a news anchor's voice as we go to vote. Each of these voices will shift attention to different aspects of a situation.

We form patterns or automatic habits about what we notice as we continue to pay attention to similar things over time. This automatic thinking about where to focus goes on without much conscious attention from us, unless we choose to bring it more fully into our awareness. We compete with these existing voices and stories when we choose to notice something new or different.

A supposedly true short story came through my e-mail that illustrates how our underlying beliefs and assumptions determine what we notice in a situation. A mother was driving her 5-year old son to school. As they approached a stop-light, the woman in the convertible in front of them stood up and waved – totally naked. The mother gasped, not sure what to say to her son. The boy exclaimed, "Mommy, that lady is not wearing her seat belt!" The mother and son were clearly paying attention to different aspects of the situation based on their underlying beliefs and assumptions. The voice of her son caused the woman to shift her attention to something very different in the situation. Had the mother said something before the boy did about the woman's appearance, the boy's understanding of the situation would have shifted with his focus. This is an overt example of co-constructing, where what we choose to notice and then ultimately construct is influenced by others.

In Western culture there is high value placed on problem-solving and critical thinking, and many view the world through this lens. There is an underlying assumption that problems exist out there that will cause harm or even death if we do not fix them. If we operate from this assumption, then what we pay attention to in a given situation are problems, or what is wrong. The habit is strong since we believe our very survival depends on it. The more we believe in the "underlying problem" assumption, the more likely we are to be critical or problem-focused in a given situation.

Appreciative Inquiry operates from a different set of assumptions. If we operate from the assumptions of the Poetic Principle, that life is open to infinite interpretations and that what we focus on creates our reality, then it makes sense to focus on the most life-affirming aspects of a situation. This brings us to look for things we like in an experience or person:

what has worked in the past, what we want in the future, and what strengths and assets are available to us. It is to assume that each situation contains tremendous positive potential if we choose to find it. This is a radical departure from the Western, problem-focused paradigm.

Shifting Beliefs

The implications of this principle are powerful. It may sound simple enough to look for the good, but shifting our automatic habits of seeing and challenging all those present and pre-existing voices and stories can be difficult. As we described earlier, our beliefs and assumptions play an important role in keeping our lives manageable. It would be impossible for us to immediately throw out all our problem-focused beliefs and replace them with AI beliefs. The transition time in changing our underlying thinking provides a buffer for us in maintaining some continuity and stability in our lives. The more steeped in problem-solving we are, the longer it can take.

There are a variety of theories and techniques for shifting our underlying beliefs and assumptions. Positive psychology spokesman Martin Seligman has a number of suggestions for creating more optimistic beliefs in his book *Authentic Happiness*. These include disputing negative beliefs, and finding less destructive ways to see a situation. [6] AI suggests that the beliefs and stories which limit our perspective can shift indirectly as we begin to focus on what we want.

Whatever We Focus on, Grows

People become what they think about, most of the time. ~Earl Nightingale

A second assumption of the Poetic Principle is that whatever we pay attention to grows, or becomes a larger part of our experience. Cooperrider and Whitney explain that "human systems grow in the direction of their deepest and most frequent inquiries."[7] Mac Odell, a leading AI practitioner, puts it this way: "If you focus on problems, you find more problems. If you focus on successes, you find more successes."[8] Again, this assumption suggests that we don't just observe reality, but create it through our acts of observation. In this way, what we focus on "grows" as we continue to notice more and more of it, expanding it into more of our reality.

Focus is Fateful

Certain branches of quantum mechanics have been exploring the idea of how we create reality by what we pay attention to. Physicist John Archibald Wheeler is one proponent of a concept called the *participative universe*,[9] which suggests that what we choose to notice in a situation becomes our reality and everything else goes by the proverbial wayside. Wheatley explains:

> [The participative universe is]…a place where the act of looking for certain information evokes the information we went looking for—and simultaneously eliminates our opportunity to observe other information…we create not only the present with our observations, but the past as well. It is the existence of observers who notice what is going on that imparts reality to everything. When we choose to experiment for one aspect, we lose our ability to see any others. Every act of measurement loses more information than it gains, closing the box irretrievably and forever on other potentials.[10]

This is the quantum physics way of saying that we have an unlimited number of ways we can create our current reality, but our decision to select one creates it and eliminates all others.[11]

Our collective choice about what to observe is not a neutral event.

Cooperrider explains this in AI as "topic choice is fateful." It speaks to this notion that what we choose to study or to notice in an organization creates that very thing. If we choose to study success we will not only find it, but more success will be generated. The same is true in our personal lives. *What we choose to pay attention to becomes a greater part of our experience.*

John Walter and Jane Peller state that, "Our belief is that whatever clients call their attention to begins to happen more often. This happens in both positive and negative ways."[12] They go on to provide an example of how this works in parenting:

> We have all seen how parents who may be very vulnerable to the fear of their teens getting into drugs become hyper-vigilant for any signs of their teen becoming involved with drugs. Through the hyper-vigilance, both the parents' attention and the teens' attention are drawn to drugs. Soon, in many cases, the parent's worst fear takes place. The opposite is also true. By shifting our attention and vigilance to what we want, the positive outcome we desire is more likely to happen.[13]

The implications of this are extensive. We are creating our experience in each moment by virtue of what we choose to pay attention to. The more attention we give something, the more it grows. This is why AI believes that problems are not the best place to focus. We are actually making them bigger with our attention.

Thinking Spirals

Minister Bill Turner coined the phrase "thoughts have babies" to capture the essence of the idea that what we focus on grows.

This phrase describes the spiraling effect of our attention as we start down a trail of noticing what is or is not working. One thought leads to another which leads to another, and the next thing we know we have traveled far down a path that defines our truth about a particular topic. We can spiral up or down or go in circles.

This happened to me recently after facilitating a large group AI session for a successful organization. I presented the exciting images of the future that came out of the data, only to be met with a response best characterized as flat. I had done this process four other times, all with incredible participant response and energy. The next day I began reflecting on what had gone wrong to try to understand what had happened (problem-focused thinking dies hard). I realized that the organization was doing so well, that the visions we created for the future were not very stimulating. People felt like they were already doing many of these great things, and were confused about what was a current strength or future possibility. Once I analyzed the flat-energy problem, I began to tear apart the rest of the meeting. I systematically critiqued any aspect of the presentation that fell short and looked for places to assign blame. Next thing I knew, I believed the meeting was a failure, and I as well for orchestrating it. Old feelings of inadequacy popped-up and I spent almost two days feeling disappointed. This is an embarrassingly good example of negative spiraling from problem focus. Had I stopped here, I would have carried a belief with me into the future that this meeting was a disaster. More importantly, I may have missed out on the inherent learning it contained.

I was so deep in the muck that it did not occur to me to apply the principles of AI until a few days later. One morning I decided to list all the good things that came out of the meeting and the entire process. The attendees were generally happy with the results and the head of the organization was very satisfied. I realized my expectations were much higher than the expectations of anyone else.

I then recalled a difficult past experience that was of tremendous value. I almost destroyed my college sorority when I became president by trying to implement big changes without group buy-in. I learned the importance of involvement and seeking input and was able to build the organization back up by the end of the semester. I looked at this learning and how it has served me over and over again, despite the pain involved.

I considered this recent meeting within the context of appreciating the inherent lessons and knew that I would be better from the experience. This feeling of gratitude allowed me to be open to learning in a way I could not when feeling down. I came to see that greater involvement of the members in the creation of the initial vision would have boosted the energy in this situation. I listed other positive aspects and learnings and was able to spiral back up and appreciate the meeting for the insight and value it provided.

Finding the Good

It is important to point out in this example that I did not ignore or gloss over the areas that fell short, or paint a perfect picture of the meeting. I looked at the meeting honestly with an appreciative eye, instead of a critical one. In this case it meant inquiring into it with a sincere and grateful intention to really learn from and discover something new from the experience. I sincerely wanted to know how to do it better the next time, and welcomed the opportunity to grow. This is a completely different focus than looking for mistakes and getting upset that I did something wrong. It is more than just semantics. It is a sincere intention to find what we want; to find something empowering and helpful in the situation.

Our feelings can provide guidance as to whether we are heading up or down the proverbial spiral. If we feel good, we're on our way up the spiral. If we feel bad, there is a good chance we are focusing on something we do not want, like, or appreciate. Again, this does not mean ignoring what is going on in the moment. It means shifting our attention to find more of what we want in the negative situation. It often requires a shift to notice and appreciate the inherent learning that is always present.

Let us circle back to the question of reality. So, was it a good or bad meeting? Was I putting on rose-colored glasses or distorting reality when I shifted my focus? To find the answer, we must go back to the Constructionist Principle. There is no "truth" about what happened in that meeting, only my interpretation of it. Each person will have experienced it differently and have formed a different opinion about how good or bad it was. The point is not to debate the "truth" about the meeting. Weick suggests that instead we focus on effectiveness, ask reflective questions of what happened, and determine what actions might have served us better.[14]

The Poetic Principle is about shifting attention in the moment to what you want. This is at the heart of AI and what sets it apart from positive thinking. It is a sincere and continuous search for the best of what is present in each moment, person, and experience. It is not what we wish were there, but the good we can actually find.

As we briefly described in the previous section, a lot of our choices about what to focus on happen automatically. This was certainly the case for me as I immediately focused on where and how the meeting broke down. We can, however, learn to shift our automatic thinking to place attention on what we want instead of problems.

Finding What We Want More of, Not Less

I do not seek, I find. ~Pablo Picasso

The third assumption of the Poetic Principle is that we can be more deliberate in finding, and hence creating, what we want. AI is about the co-evolutionary search for the best in people, their organizations, and the relevant world around them.[15] It is not about searching for people who are not at their worst, as silly as this may sound. We can only create what we want more of, not less of.

Think "To" Rather than Think "From"

Focusing our attention on what we do want will create more of it, while focusing on what we don't want will create more of that as well. If we focus on how we "never have enough money," what we create in our lives is "not enough money." Psychiatrist Milton Erickson claimed it was not possible to create a mental image or think about not doing something.[16] For example, if I tell you not to think about a pink flamingo, you will have already created an image of it as I speak. The more I tell you not to think about it, the more I call your attention to it. It is our attention to something that makes it part of our experience.

It would be much easier if I told you to think about a purple crocodile, instead of not thinking about a pink flamingo. Notice how much easier it is to not think about the pink flamingo when there is something else to focus on. The inherent assumption in this idea is that you know what you want. Many of us know we do not want pink flamingoes but don't have a clear vision of what we truly desire. It can be difficult to determine what we do want when we have automatic habits of paying attention to problems, or what we don't want.

Walter and Peller describe this in discussing a drinking problem with a client:

> The more the conversation is drawn to talking of the problem, the more the client and therapist are thinking of and associating further about the problem… The more a conversation is focused on not-drinking as a problem or as a preference, the

> more both client and consultant are thinking of
> drinking…What makes more sense, both
> pragmatically and metaphorically, is to think of
> something else. What makes even more sense is to
> think of what we want to happen or what we want in
> our life rather than trying to stop thinking about or
> eradicating what we do not want.[17]

Another way to think about this is that it is much more
powerful to *think to,* rather than *think from.* "Thinking to"
involves creating images and ideas about what we want, and
"thinking from" is looking at how we can eliminate or fix
something we don't want. "Thinking to" is a creative act and
"thinking from" is destructive.

As we discussed above, it can be difficult to shift our
automatic ways of seeing to focus on what we want. One way
to do this is by asking different questions, which we will
discuss at length in the chapter on the Simultaneity Principle. A
second way to do this is with a technique professor and
consultant Gervase Bushe calls "tracking and fanning."[18]

Tracking and Fanning

Tracking and fanning is a technique for finding what we want
in a person or situation and then magnifying it. In his book
Clear Leadership, Bushe describes tracking as, "the ability to
see what we want more of as already being there."[19] It is
finding love in a person you dislike, or deeper love in someone
you care about. It is seeing generosity in someone selfish,
finding peace amidst chaos, and discovering joy in turbulent
times. It requires a belief in the assumptions of the Poetic
Principle—that all is present in a person or situation—and
looking for what we want brings it to life.

Bushe tells an interesting story in his book about a team
led by a man named Jack, who handled a difficult situation
with an African warlord. The story nicely illustrates the use of

tracking and fanning and his publisher, Davies-Black, kindly permitted it to be reprinted here:

> A team from Healthy World, a non-governmental organization, had entered the small, war-torn African country to get permission from the current ruler to allow them to begin inoculating children against diarrhea, one of the major causes of infant mortality. There were reports that government forces were killing women and children in outlying villages, and just before the audience with the ruler someone had put a videotape into Jack's hands, showing a recent massacre. The irony of inoculating children who might then be gunned down was not lost on Jack, the team leader, and he decided to try and do something about it.

> When he was given an audience with the ruler, he explained their desire to inoculate the children and asked for permission to do so, which he was given. He then also asked the ruler if he would help to open the first clinic to begin "saving the children of your country." The ruler agreed to do that. Then, in a risky move, Jack asked for a videotape machine and played the tape of the ruler's troops massacring women and children. Nothing more was said except to thank the ruler for having given his permission to "save the children of your country."

> A few days later when the outdoor clinic was set up and mothers were lined up with children to get the inoculations, the Healthy World staff put the syringe in the ruler's hands and invited him to give the injections. As the long line of thankful mothers, joyful over the blessing they were receiving at the hand of their ruler, moved past, the Healthy World staff kept saying to him, "You are saving the children of your country. Now you really are the father of your nation." The ruler so enjoyed himself

> he decided to cancel all his engagements and spent
> the next few weeks traveling with the clinic
> throughout the country, personally inoculating
> children and being reminded over and over that
> "now you really are the father of your nation." The
> massacres stopped.[20]

As this story illustrates, when we begin to look for, or "track" the attribute we want, it begins to grow larger. At first, the attribute we want may be quite small, or even impossible to see. Bushe says sometimes it requires a "leap of faith" to believe that it exists in the first place. In the story above, it took a leap of faith to find caring and compassion in the African ruler. For us, it might be noticing what's right with our rude neighbor, or finding good in a person who burglarized our home. But if we believe it's there, and keep looking, eventually we will find it. When we do, we can begin "fanning" like crazy.

"Fanning" is what Bushe refers to as the process of magnifying what we want.[21] It involves finding ways to appreciate and affirm the good, which makes it grow larger. It is a form of positive reinforcement as we notice, appreciate, and call attention to what we want in the moment. We are fanning when we offer praise for a job well done: to our children when they behave well, to a spouse who has been helpful, to ourselves when we have been kind and thoughtful. Fanning can also be done more formally by giving awards, sending gifts, or thank-you cards. By sincerely acknowledging and affirming whatever is wanted, we reinforce that behavior or attribute.

Tracking and Fanning Examples

Parents and teachers have been embracing this concept for some time. There are many books on positive reinforcement for finding what we want in our children and then encouraging that behavior. A story from *The Right Questions* by Debbie Ford illustrates the use of tracking and fanning to deal with a common child behavior problem:

> …When Erin [Jonathan's mother] arrived at Jonathan's school one day, his teacher made an offhand remark about Jonathan's habit of picking his nose. Erin was horrified…As she grew more preoccupied with her son's bad habit, Erin seemed to lose sight of the bigger picture—that she was blessed with a healthy, funny, creative, and loving child. The more Erin reprimanded Jonathan for his actions, the more he acted out, sometimes picking his nose right in front of her just to gain attention.
>
> Finally, when Erin realized she was just focusing on what was wrong with her son, she decided to give up trying to fix his behavior and instead focus her attention on all the things that were right about Jonathan. At bedtime after she read him his good-night story, Erin began stroking his head and telling him all the things she loved about him. Within a few days Jonathan had stopped acting out and instead seemed to be thriving in the presence of his mother's approval. [22]

This story illustrates how Erin was able to track more of the behavior she wanted in her son, and then fan it by talking about it with him at night. There were two parts to the success of this endeavor. The first was her sincere attention to and appreciation of the attributes she wanted to see, and the second was letting go of attention to what was not wanted. In the same book, Ford asks us to consider:

> What would happen if we listened to our neighbors as though they were the wisest people in the world? Would they show up any different than they do right now? What would be possible if we approached our

> partners as though their sole purpose was to bring us
> ecstasy and joy? What would we hear? What would
> we see? What would be possible? Looking for
> what's right is a life-enhancing choice—a choice
> that promises peace, contentment, and fulfillment.[23]

Consider how our lives would change if we began shifting our focus to the good.

Gratitude

Gratitude is another powerful way to help automatically re-direct our thinking to focus on what is right. The value of creating gratitude lists has been touted by a variety of people and institutions from Oprah Winfrey to various twelve-step programs. The essential idea is to spend time each day focusing attention on what we are grateful for. If we intentionally look for what is right or working in our lives, we will begin to create more of it.

Martin Seligman and others have documented the benefits of gratitude.[24] In one experiment, he had participants write three good things (big or small) that happened to them every day for one week, and list why they thought this good thing happened. He found that people were happier and less depressed immediately after doing the activity, and the positive effects were still being experienced three months later.[25]

Gratitude is one of the most powerful ways to shift our thinking to focus on the good and create more of it in our lives. It helps train our minds to automatically notice what we want more of. When I first tried using a gratitude list many years ago, I had a hard time coming up with items. On particularly bad days, I reached for things to be grateful for, and listed things such as having toilet paper. I found that as I did the practice more, it became easier to come up with items. There was definitely a learning curve for me in learning to find the good, and it still continues.

Shifting our focus to tracking and fanning, "thinking to" what we want, or simply becoming aware of our gratitude are some of the most powerful ways to incrementally change our lives. It is like changing the course of a large ship by one degree. At first the trajectory does not look much different, but over time the gap widens and our lives end up in a completely different place.

Developing an "Appreciative Eye"

Thus the task is not so much to see what no one yet has seen, but to think what nobody yet has thought about that which everybody sees. ~Schopenhauer

Cooperrider explains that the appreciative eye "apprehends 'what is' rather than 'what is not' and...not only draws our eye toward life, but stirs our feelings, excites our curiosity and provides inspiration to the envisioning mind."[26] He explains that affirmation is the first step in appreciation, and that as we appreciate we generate new ways of knowing.

Affirming Versus Appreciating

We describe or acknowledge what is already there when we affirm something. For example, an affirmation of a painting might be that it has excellent composition, or that we like it. We might affirm that we are good cooks, or that a friend has good taste in clothes. We get to appreciation by taking affirmation to the next level.

Appreciating goes beyond affirming by inquiring deeper into the positive aspects of something. *Affirmation is descriptive and appreciation is creative.*[27] The artisan reproduces, and the artist creates.[28] Hungarian biochemist

Albert Szent-Gyorgyi said, "Discovery consists of seeing what everybody has seen and thinking what no one else has thought."

Appreciating is a more open and generative way of experiencing what is present. As we discussed earlier, life experience is rich. There are an infinite number of things we can notice and ways we can construct meaning in each moment. When we appreciate, we are inspired to inquire into what we like, and our curiosity causes us to notice new things. It is almost as if we call forth greater possibility by our belief and desire to see it so. We take a more active role in cognitively molding what we experience into new possibilities that transform how we think.

In the painting example, we might begin by affirming that it is well-composed, and then become curious about that and inquire more deeply into it. We might ponder the artist's use of contrast, and the way it seems to make the light "dance" off the canvas. This might lead us to new thoughts about the use of contrast and movement in art, or any host of other creative thoughts about technique, style, or talent.

Physicist David Bohm suggests that "creativity...is always founded on the sensitive perception of what is new and different from what is inferred from previous knowledge."[29] In this way, appreciation is creative, as it represents new positive ways of thinking or perceiving. As we discussed in the Constructionist Principle, we create our reality through our thoughts. As we discover new and more wonderful ways of knowing, we create more wonderful ways of being.

One of the essential components in developing an appreciative eye is the ability to focus so exclusively on the positive that the negative becomes irrelevant. It may sound like having an appreciative eye is like wearing rose-colored glasses, but there is a difference. Consider Cooperrider's account of Winston Churchill's ability to see the positive:

> Churchill's impact and the guiding images he helped
> create were the result of his towering ability to
> cognitively dissociate all seeming impossibilities,
> deficiencies, and imperfections from a given
> situation and to see in his people and country that
> which had fundamental value and strength. His
> optimism, even in Britain's darkest moment, came
> not from a Pollyanna-like sense that "everything is
> just fine" but from a conviction that was born from
> what he, like few others, could actually see in his
> country: "Doubtless it was there; but largely
> dormant until he had awoken it."[30]

Wearing rose-colored glasses is analogous to ignoring negative aspects or pretending they don't exist. The Appreciative eye sees and believes in the positive side so strongly, it overshadows the negative elements.

Our Senses are Socially Conditioned

Social conditioning plays an active role in determining what we consider to be the positive and negative elements. I remember being in Australia and eating the popular food "vegemite" for the first time. I did not like the taste at all, and asked my Australian friend if it was really as popular as I had heard. She responded that it was, and asked if that awful-tasting peanut butter was really as popular in the US as we claimed. We had a laugh as we realized how taste was socially-conditioned. Our other senses are socially-conditioned as well. What we learn to find tasteful, pleasant, and beautiful is socially constructed.

Barry Kaufman describes a poem he read about gnarled, bent trees that had been "beaten into submission" by the wind at the ocean's edge. He went to the same place with an appreciative eye, and came to a new and beautiful understanding of how miraculous the trees were in adapting and flowing with the force of the wind. He explains that "what some might depict as a struggle is actually the silent inner dance of a tree moving synergistically with the wind in a demonstration of perfect harmony and suitability."[31]

One of the best ways we can learn to enjoy and appreciate new things is through the eyes of another. People who love music, opera, the subway, fast food, old cars, or rap music can show us what they appreciate, and we can learn through them if we are open to new ways of knowing. We are continuously in conversations with others, which provide a wonderful way for us to continue to expand our notions of what is pleasant, wonderous, and beautiful. The following paraphrased story by Roger Dean Kiser, Sr. illustrates this idea further:

> Once upon a time there was a little orphan boy who wanted to fly and a little crippled boy who wished he could walk and run. The crippled boy's father took him to the park, and the two boys met. The orphan boy asked the other if he had ever wanted to fly like a bird. "No," said the boy who could not walk or run. "But I have wondered what it would be like to walk and run like other boys and girls."

> The two boys played together for hours. The orphan boy said to the other, "I wish there was something I could do to make you walk and run like other little boys and girls, but I can't. But there is something I can do for you. Slide up onto my back."

> And so, the little boy slid up on his friend's back. Then the orphan boy began to run across the grass. Faster and harder he ran across the park. Soon the wind whistled across the two little boys faces.

> The little boy's father began to cry as he watched his beautiful little crippled son flapping his arms up and down in the wind, all the while yelling at the top of his voice, "I'm flying Daddy, I'm flying![32]

Each of these boys was able to experience life through the eyes of the other, and enjoy a realm of life that would have otherwise gone unnoticed. Some of the greatest moments can be found in tapping into the joy experienced by another. If you want to watch someone come alive, inquire deeply into something she is excited about, and earnestly try to experience through her senses. Put yourself in her place and inquire into her experience until you begin to feel some of the same excitement. It's a great way to help develop an appreciative eye, and to connect more deeply with another.

There are aspects in every moment and person to appreciate, and a large part of our ability to do this is cognitive. Even though we experience through our senses, our sensorial experience is formed by the meaning we attach and where we choose to focus. When we recognize that the things we enjoy and appreciate are another form of social construction, we can deliberately look for new ways of seeing and appreciating.

The essence of the appreciative eye is inhabiting a spirit of curiosity and openness to more positive ways of sensing and knowing. Just like good wine, good food, and good music, what we have come to like in people is socially constructed. When we open ourselves to new understandings, we can re-construct our images in ways that are more reflective of what we want to experience. This applies to people, present experiences, past memories and future images. In the Simultaneity Principle chapter we'll further explore what it means to live in this spirit of wonder.

Final Thoughts

The Poetic Principle suggests that people and life experience are rich with positive potential. We have creative license to poetically describe and construct each experience with others any way we desire. The more we give attention to something, whether we want it or not, the more it grows. Affirmations are one way to acknowledge the good, but we can take affirming one step further by appreciating. We can develop an "appreciative eye" by inhabiting a spirit of openness and curiosity in our lives, which creates new and more positive ways of knowing.

Computer giant Microsoft asks, "Where do you want to go today?"™ The Internet, like life experience, lies at our fingertips before us, rich with potential, all things present. Our choice about what to enter in the address field creates our internet experience. Our choice about what to focus on in each moment creates our life experience.

CHAPTER 3

The Simultaneity Principle

Quality questions create a quality life.

~ ANTHONY ROBBINS

The Simultaneity Principle rests in the power of inquiry, and suggests that change begins the moment we ask a question.[1] Cooperrider and Whitney describe the fundamental nature of questions in Appreciative Inquiry (AI):

> AI involves, in a central way, the art and practice of asking questions that strengthen a system's capacity to apprehend, anticipate, and heighten positive potential. It centrally involves the mobilization of inquiry through the crafting of the "unconditional positive question..."[2]

An underlying spirit of wonder and curiosity sets AI apart from simple appreciative perspectives, and as Rainer Maria Rilke said, we learn "to love the questions themselves." Our understandings, beliefs, and images evolve and change simultaneously as we seek to discover ourselves and the world through questions. There are no "neutral" questions; every inquiry takes us somewhere, even if it is back to what we originally believed. Inhabiting this spirit of wonder can transform our lives, and the unconditional positive question is one of the greatest tools we have to this end.

We Live in the World Our Questions Create

Change Your Questions, Change Your Life.[3]
~Marilee Adams

The AI book *Encyclopedia of Positive Questions* states that "people live in the worlds their questions create."[4] The internal and external questions we ask steer our thinking, attention, and images in one direction or another, which in turn directs our decisions and creates our experience. There is a saying that goes something like, "If you keep doing what you always did, you'll keep getting what you always got." In the same vein, if we continue to ask the same questions, we'll continue to create the same world. We have patterns of thinking that tend to lead us down similar questioning paths.

We Continuously Ask Questions

As we engage in an average day we are continually asking and answering questions. How do I look today? Why does Bill look so mad? What will I work on next? Who is driving that car? Our inner dialogue goes on and on. These constant questions and the answers we produce incrementally direct our attention and create our experience for that day.

Consider a small sample of many possible questions upon the first few minutes of waking. Should I hit the snooze alarm or get up now? Am I looking forward to this day or am I wishing it away? What will I do first, second, third, etc.? If we reflect on this thinking process, we realize each of our choices was an answer to an implicit question. For example, our decision about what to eat for breakfast came from an internal question that might have been, "What do I feel like eating today?" Or perhaps it was, "What's in the kitchen I can eat quickly for breakfast today?"

Consider what would happen if we asked one different question in the morning such as, "What would be the healthiest thing I could eat this morning that would leave me feeling good about myself and give me the greatest energy to start the day?" Even if we made the same breakfast choice, it would be done with a different mindset. If we continued to ask this same new question each morning, at some point we would begin to change our actions by virtue of our attention. As we discussed in the Poetic Principle, whatever we focus on begins to grow. Our continual questions about and attention to health and energy would begin to create change in that area. Therapist Marilee Adams explains:

> If you ask the Right Questions before you make a choice, you will shift yourself away from automatic, repetitive cycles and toward deliberate, focused steps that will lead you toward the future you desire. The Right Questions penetrate your denial system and wake you up.[5]

A lot of our internal dialogue goes unnoticed since many of the questions we ask ourselves occur automatically. Walter & Peller explain how the language of the question, the assumptions within the question, and even the answers are already mediated by the beliefs within the community of inquirers.[6] Our questions emerge from co-created patterns we have developed along the way through life experience. For example, if we lived in a third world country our underlying belief might be there is not enough food. Our automatic question about breakfast might be whether or not there is any.

Issues of health and weight would also be questioned from a very different perspective.

The question and answer "habits" that guide our lives are continuously streaming through our brain all day long, and it is not possible to monitor every one. As explained earlier, our automatic thinking habits serve important functions in keeping our lives manageable. If we had to consciously construct every question and answer in a day we would be overwhelmed. What we can do is realize these thought processes are going on, appreciate the value they provide, and make a point to ask questions in a more intentional way at appropriate times.

Questions Create Our Experience

In addition to internal questions, we are also asking and being asked external questions. Consider the difference in asking a friend about her day. An AI approach might include, "What was the best part of your day today?" or "What went well for you today?" A more middle-of-the-road question might be, "How was your day today?" or "How did it go today?" A problem-focused question might be, "How did you survive your day today?" or "Did you make it through your day today?" Each of these questions would generate slightly different meanings, and take the conversation to a different place. In the Poetic Principle I discussed how thinking can spiral up or down, and conversations can do the same thing. Continued questions from the same perspective could begin spiraling the discussion in one direction or another, leaving you both feeling one extreme or another about her day.

In addition to these more typical daily questions, there are more profound questions such as "What do you value most about your self?" or "What are your three greatest wishes for your future?" These types of questions can reach into deeper areas of our lives and affect more sweeping personal changes. A more problem-saturated version of these questions would be "What are your weakest areas?" or "What are the three biggest areas of your life that need improvement?" If we believe in the principles of AI then asking about our wishes and strengths will lead to greater positive change than asking about what is broken.

AI assumes that human systems grow in the direction of what they persistently ask questions about.[7] The more we continue to inquire into an area, the richer and deeper our constructions become. Our questions become our experience.

Change Begins the Moment We Question

All questions are leading questions.
~Michael Hoyt

The very first questions we ask in a situation influence the meaning that is made, the images we construct, and the actions we take. One mantra of the Simultaneity Principle is that *inquiry and change are simultaneous.* Cooperrider & Whitney explain that "the seeds of change—that is, the things people think and talk about, the things people discover and learn, and the things that inform dialogue and inspire images of the future—are implicit in the very first questions we ask."[8]

The first questions we ask in a situation are particularly important, since we form initial thoughts and beliefs, or "impressions," that tend to frame our thinking going forward. Questions are openings for creating something new. Harrison Owen believes "the most helpful thing is not the answer, which all people must find for themselves. It is the question that sets the ball in motion."[9] Whitney & Trosten-Bloom explain:

> Questions can stimulate ideas, innovation, and invention. New knowledge, theories, and inventions have frequently evolved from unusual questions....Many scientists and inventors tell of the question that "haunted" them, begging for resolution

until the answer emerged and along with it a new
idea, or invention.[10]

Well-known biologist Rupert Sheldrake told Otto Scharmer
how he chose biology for love of animals. Once he got into the
field, he discovered it was more about killing and dissecting
them. He said a defining moment occurred for him when he
asked and became driven by the new question, "What would it
take to develop a science that enhances life?"[11] Sheldrake
generated several innovative ideas from this question,
including "morphic fields," discussed in the Constructionist
Principle.

When we desire change from our "typical" way of being,
we need to become more aware of the questions we are asking.
If we begin to ask new questions we'll begin to see observable
changes in our life in response to those questions. We can
become more deliberate in using questions to help create the
space for more productive, constructive conversations and
relationships with others. Cooperrider & Whitney explain:

> It is not so much "Is my question leading to right or
> wrong answers?" but rather "What impact is my
> question having on our lives together…is it helping
> to generate conversations about the good, the better,
> the possible…is it strengthening our relationships?[12]

Questions drive the conversations we have with others, which
drive the relationships we create. In a previous example we
discussed the different ways we can ask a friend about her day.
Our choice will set a conversation in motion and direct our
attention and feelings about each other accordingly. From this
perspective *it becomes less about finding the exact right
question and more about finding a question that takes us to the
right places.*

The changes resulting from our questions are not all
outwardly apparent. Change is an incremental, continuous

process that occurs on many levels. Often we think of change as a fixed event that occurs after a relatively large, observable difference has emerged. We notice our co-worker has lost weight since we saw him two weeks ago, and ask about this change. In actuality his weight changes constantly, and as we speak he is burning calories. His beliefs, decisions, and actions regarding his weight are all also changing continuously.

We are in a constant state of regeneration, and our questions help direct us accordingly. Since our questions are co-constructed, we have the ability to change them. As we continue to intentionally shift our questions, we eventually form new question "habits." One of the better habits we can form is in learning to ask positive questions.

The Unconditional Positive Question

Change the way you look at things and the things you look at change. ~Wayne Dyer

Questions can be used for many purposes such as gaining information, manipulating, showing understanding, providing insight, and a variety of other things. In Appreciative Inquiry we pay particular attention to the power of questions in creating change. The unconditional positive question is believed to be the most powerful means to this end. The AI *Encyclopedia of Positive Questions* provides one definition of this type of question:

> A positive question is an affirmatively stated question—a question that seeks to uncover and bring out the best in a person, a situation or an organization. It is constructed around a topic that…is fundamentally affirmative.[13]

The unconditional positive question asks about times when things are at their best. It engenders a sense of wonder, excitement, and inspiration around the topic of focus. It is *generative*, in that it stimulates new thinking that takes us beyond our current ways of knowing. It asks us to look at what's right, what works, and what we want most. It often involves asking about the *positive core*, which contains the wisdom, successful strategies, best practices, skills, resources, and capabilities of a person or organization."[14]

Positive questions can be as simple as, "What went well today?" or "What do you like about this book so far?" These are typical questions we might ask within the course of a normal day. They help shift attention to the positive side of a topic. We can also ask more elaborate positive questions that inspire more in-depth thinking and discovery. For example, "As you reflect on your day today, what stands out as one of the high points, and why was it a high point for you?" or, "As you think about the reading you've done up to this point, what is it you like most about this book and why?" These questions generate deeper exploration and cause greater shifts in knowing. They not only shift attention to the positive, but they take us further into the construction of it.

Finally, there are full-scale positive questions that contain an introduction and/or follow-up. These types of questions create bigger shifts in our perspective and open new doors of possibility. They have the capacity to re-construct and re-author our stories and lives in significant ways through their asking and answering.

Full-Scale Positive Questions

In the following two paragraphs, I've put together a full-scale unconditional positive question on the above example of what went well today. The first paragraph contains an inspirational poem to create a positive tone, and the second paragraph contains the actual question. Consider how this question might stimulate new thinking for you in ways the scaled-down versions did not:

> Author Mary Jean Iron writes: *"Normal day, let me be aware of the treasure you are. Let me learn from you, love you, bless you before you depart. Let me not pass you by in quest of some rare and perfect tomorrow. Let me hold you while I may, for it may not always be so. One day I shall dig my nails into the earth, ...or raise my hands to the sky and want, more than all the world, your return."*

> Some days of our lives are filled with great fanfare, though many are simple and gentle in their passing. Each day offers the potential to see common life in miraculous new ways, and discover beauty in the ordinary. As singer and songwriter Joni Mitchell wrote, "You don't know what you've got till it's gone." While you read and ponder these paragraphs, the seconds and minutes pass, life passes. As you reflect on the gift of your "average" day today, what is it that you appreciate? If this were your last day here on Earth and you could hold on to one aspect of it, what would it be and why?

Hopefully you can see and feel the difference in this type of question from the others that were less involved. Full-scale positive questions take us *beyond* the positive and into more expansive thinking. The inspirational thought at the beginning helps us feel grateful for what we might currently be experiencing as a routine or boring day. There are several statements throughout that challenge an automatic assumption most of us carry that we will be alive beyond today. Questioning this assumption jars our thinking and creates new opportunities for constructing what's possible. Additional follow-up questions could be added to further test our underlying assumptions and create more possibility for change.

Research shows that the more positive the question we ask, the more long-term the change.[15]

Crafting a full-scale positive question is like creating a work of art, and there are three characteristics that set these questions apart from others. First is the poetic use of language in articulating an inspiring, relevant, affirmative image of what exists and/or is wanted. The initial part of the question is aimed at creating an appreciative mindset about the affirmative topic. Positive emotion is a critical factor in the success of this endeavor. The stronger our emotions are around something, the more powerful our movement toward it.[16]

The second characteristic of the full-scale question is that it is grounded in reality. It asks about actual past and present peak experiences and strengths rather than simply talking about a hypothetical ideal. If we talk about actual ideal experiences, no matter how fleeting they may be, we go forward with a belief it can happen again since it has already occurred at least once in some form. Ideal experiences also provide relevant information for the conditions that caused success. Situating AI within lived experience is what sets it apart from positive thinking. When we do ask about an ideal hypothetical future, it is done within the context of successful past experiences.

The final characteristic of the full-scale positive question is the ability to stage a compelling, positive inquiry into a positive possibility that challenges current assumptions. There is a mouthful. Essentially it is the art of creating questions that "sneak up on us" by implicitly pushing the envelope of our assumptions. The above example innocently suggests a "what-if" scenario, where today is our last day here on earth. Shifting our underlying assumptions about our future and death creates new perspectives.

Cooperrider suggests, based on the work of Henry Wieman, that our most limiting assumptions are actually positive in nature.[17] For example, we might assume that being happy most of the time is about as good as we can expect our lives to be. This assumption might be well below what is possible. If we don't believe it's possible to regularly experience states of high joy, then this limits our ability to do so. We often aspire to ideals that are inadequate.[18] A compelling inquiry is one that takes us willingly into the discovery of new images that transform our beliefs and assumptions of what is possible.

AI Questionnaires

The *Encyclopedia of Positive Questions*[19] provides more details about how to craft positive questions for organizations and gives several examples. A questionnaire, or "interview protocol" as it is called, is typically created in organizations for people to ask and answer a variety of positive questions. We can make up questionnaires for our personal lives as well. These would typically contain questions about such things as peak experiences, high points, strengths, values, and best practices. Such questions create a positive stage from which a later question is often asked about wishes for the future.

I like to end a questionnaire with a practical question asking what small change we could make now that would move us towards the future we desire. We'll discuss more about small changes in the Anticipatory Principle chapter, but the essential idea is that big changes begin small. It's a great way to take the ideas generated during the questioning and begin action towards the desired future.

We can also include questions that address problems, as a way to "bridge" to AI. These types of questions help us focus on what we want within the comfort zone of our problems. For example, we might imagine that a difficult situation has miraculously resolved, and ask what led to the resolution, and/or what is different about life now without this problem. Or, we might think of a time in the past when the problem did not exist when it normally would, or we were able to deal with it successfully. We would then inquire into the conditions that led to success during those times.

The purpose of the questionnaire is not so much to gather information as to create new meaning and beliefs within the conversation that move our thinking forward. We can also study successes and strengths in an effort to learn more about what works, but it is the process of talking, internally and externally, about these experiences and practices that brings them in as part of our learning, thinking, and reality. This is why the interview itself is of great value in an AI intervention, independent of what is done with the data. Change occurs inside of us in the moment of questioning and answering. This is true for both the interviewer and interviewee.

Ask for What You Want More of

It is important to ask about what we want more of, and not less. Our attention will create our experience, and if we focus on lack we create more lack. Remember the example in the Poetic Principle chapter of not thinking of a pink flamingo. Our minds cannot process the negative part of this statement, so an image of a pink flamingo inevitably shows up in our consciousness.

For example, if we are struggling financially, we need to ask questions about financial abundance. If we ask how we can eliminate financial stress or get rid of financial problems, we create more financial stress and problems. If you just try to *not* think about financial stress, your mind will still continue to go there. Trying *not* to think of something is almost like a vacuum that continues to suck you into the thought. Our minds are continuously in action, and it is not possible to simply "stop" that activity.

We need to find something else to think about, and creating an image of what we want is one way to fill that "thinking void." If I ask you to think about the times in your life when you were financially abundant, no matter how brief, your mind moves to focusing on those abundant times. Whatever we focus on grows, and this is how we create more abundance. Again, we have to ask about what we want more of, not less of.

Practical Considerations

So, how do we apply all this practically in our daily lives? Most of the time we will probably use some version of the smaller-scale positive questions in our daily internal and external conversations. Using these questions alone can create a significant change, by virtue of continuously focusing attention on what we want.

When we want to make bigger changes in our lives, it would be worth the time to develop a full-scale AI question. The designing of the question itself can be a significant part of the change. The thinking that goes into crafting the question can be as valuable as answering the question.

One other aspect of these questions that needs to be considered is the idea of collaboration. We can design and answer these questions alone, but the power of doing it with another magnifies the impact significantly. This is especially true if the people we choose will be directly impacted by the desired change. They become co-creators in the new reality.

For example, if I decide I want to change to become more loving and accepting of others (the affirmative version of being critical and judgmental) it would be helpful to involve others in my inquiry. I might ask a friend to help me craft the question, and both our perspectives will shift as we discuss what it means to be loving and accepting, what should and should not be included, what is relevant, and so on. I can then find someone I feel comfortable with to ask and answer the questions with me. It is important to have both people asking and answering some version of the question in order to deepen the connection and maximize the collaborative potential. Notice the split from the therapy model, which is typically one person asking (the therapist) and another answering (the client.)

This type of intimate conversation builds tremendous bonds between the interviewer and interviewee; our partner will likely become our greatest advocate. The more people we involve, the greater our support group. It is especially helpful to involve those whom we think might oppose the change for some reason. An appreciative dialogue is a good way to find common ground and build support for new beginnings.

David Cooperrider posted on the AI list-serve[20] that one of the most important leadership strengthening tools he knew was having leaders ask at least one different positive question each day.[21] I would suggest this is true for us in our personal lives. One of the best things we can do to help create what we want in our lives is to try to ask at least one new positive question daily.

One woman I worked with who was head of a private school said the most profound thing she learned from AI was in asking people what they want. When people came to her with problems, she used to ask for details about what was wrong and what they didn't like. *Now she asks them what they do want.* She realized that just because she knows what they don't like, or don't want, it doesn't tell her how to change things for the better. For example, she realized that if someone doesn't like the parking lot design, it doesn't necessarily mean he wants a new parking lot. She does not let people "leave her office" now until they tell her what they want. If they can't answer the question at that time, which is not uncommon, she tells them to get back to her when they do know what they want. She has come to realize she cannot initiate change until she knows what changes are desired.

AI suggests that we can create more of what we want in our lives by becoming more aware of the questions we ask. Small-scale positive questions can help us create more of what we want, and large-scale questions can help speed the process for major changes and transformation.

Living in Wonder

There are only two ways to live your life. One is as though nothing is a miracle. The other is as though everything is. ~Albert Einstein

The nature of questioning we have discussed so far has been fairly pragmatic. We've explained the mechanics of how questions direct attention and create more of whatever is being asked about, but there is a deeper level to all this. In living from a place of wonder and awe, we unleash the spirit of inquiry from deep within, where we are sincerely interested and curious about things in general. We develop a child-like sense of discovery and openness to what life presents. If we live from this place of wonder, positive questions begin to flow naturally as we eagerly inquire into the world around us.

In the article, *"The 'Child' as Agent of Inquiry,"*[22] David Cooperrider describes the nature of wonder and awe, and points out that children are naturally endowed with this ability. They explore their world with all senses fully engaged and open to whatever life presents. Life is fascinating from this perspective—alive, interesting, and always novel. Cooperrider explains how this same sense of wonder can be developed by adults as we earnestly inquire into the most positive aspects of something.

> It begins in ordinary circumstances of discovery, conversation, and the deepening relationship—all endowed by the positive question. *Inquiry itself creates wonder. When I'm really in a mode of inquiry, appreciable worlds are discovered everywhere. The feeling of wonder is the outcome. Of course it also cycles back. A good positive question, like Karl Weick's notion of "small wins," can change the world.*[23]

Cooperrider suggests that being in this state of positive inquiry facilitates our ability to see what is good, right, and miraculous about the situation or person at hand. The questions themselves can begin to foster and grow a feeling of wonder and awe as more is discovered. Learning is facilitated by this process as well. When we are sincerely curious about something, it becomes more interesting, and we are likely to ask and learn more about it. Actress Lily Tomlin cleverly suggests we practice "awe-aerobics" to exercise our capability to see the miraculous.[24]

Openness Fosters Wonder

Some therapists describe how interest builds in client conversations as they let go of their preconceived notions and open themselves more fully to what clients are saying. Therapist Michael Hoyt wrote, "The harder I listen, the smarter the client gets."[25] Harlene Anderson found that, "When we listened carefully to clients we…became interested in what they were saying."[26] Walter and Peller explain:

> If we enter a relationship assuming ahead of time
> that we know what is right or best for our clients,
> then we are already closing off possibilities, as well
> as our ability to be open and understanding. *As soon
> as we assume we understand, then curiosity
> ceases.*[italics added]…Curiosity and wonder are
> facilitated when we ask questions without an end in
> mind.[27]

Openness is a key aspect of this spirit of discovery. It is choosing a position of not-knowing. Letting go of judgments and preconceived notions is central to being present to what is emerging before us. As Walter and Peller suggest, "if we already know what's going to happen, or what it all means, it all becomes much less interesting."[28] If we "know" people, we focus less on who they are being in the moment, and our attention towards them drops. We all experience this in relationships. Our friend, partner, or spouse is not quite as interesting twenty years later as they were the first few times we met them (except, of course, for my husband.)

Again, this is all part of our automatic thinking, which is doing its best to help us out by giving us less to process in each moment. The more we know someone or something, the less time we have to spend deciding if they are safe, nice, kind, enjoyable, or beautiful, so we can put our thinking time elsewhere. We lose in novelty what we gain in mental efficiency. It takes effort to momentarily silence those automatic ways of knowing and be open to familiar things in a wonderous new way.

Developing Curiosity

Psychology professor Mihaly Csikszentmihalyi suggests four steps in developing greater personal interest and curiosity in his book, *Flow*. They are:

1) Try to be surprised by something everyday.
2) Try to surprise at least one person everyday.
3) Write down each day what surprised you and how you surprised others.
4) When something strikes a spark of interest, follow it.[29]

Cooperrider suggests another way to engage in a spirit of wonder is by adopting the metaphor of "life as a miracle."[30] If we begin to focus on the miraculous nature of everyone and everything around us, we create more miraculous people and life experiences. We can do this by asking unconditional positive questions about the miraculous nature of ourselves and our lives.

For example, we might start by asking, "How can I become more aware of the miraculous nature of life as I engage with it? In what ways would seeing the "miracles" present in everyday situations add to the quality of my life? What is it about the universe and all of life that is beyond comprehension? What is so amazing about my body that it defies understanding? What is it about the beauty of nature that leaves me breathless?

Consider how it feels when someone asks you questions about something wonderful you did, and listens in awe with rapt attention. Your heart swells and you begin to feel like you are capable of great things. We discussed this positive affirming cycle earlier in the Poetic Principle. There is something about being totally appreciated that fills something deep within us. Asking positive questions with a spirit of wonder is one of the most powerful ways of building appreciative capacity in relationships.

Wonder drives inquiry. Wonder about life's grandest and most beautiful aspects and potential is what drives Appreciative Inquiry.

Final Thoughts

All day, every day, we ask and answer question after question. The first questions we ask in a new situation frame our thinking and begin the change process. We create more of whatever we inquire into, so it is best to ask about what we want more of, not less. There is no such thing as a neutral question, and the unconditional positive question is one of the most transformational types of inquiry we can make. The underlying essence of appreciative questioning is a child-like spirit of wonder about life's grandest and most beautiful aspects and potential. The familiar saying goes, "Be careful what you ask for, because you just might get it." I would suggest instead, "Be deliberate in what you ask for, and you can create it."

CHAPTER 4

The Anticipatory Principle

The future is not a result of choices among alternate paths offered by the present, but a place that is created—created first in the mind and will, created next in activity. The future is not some place we are going to, but one we are creating. The paths are not to be found, but made, and the activity of making them changes both the maker and the destination.

~ JOHN SCHAAR

The future is part of our reality. I have described how we co-create reality in previous chapters. The Anticipatory Principle suggests that the images we create in our minds about the future guide our present actions and create that very future. Cooperrider and Whitney explain:

> One of the basic theorems of the anticipatory view of organizational life is that it is the image of the future, which in fact guides what might be called the current behavior of any organism or organization. Much like a movie projector on a screen, human systems are forever projecting ahead of themselves a horizon of expectation (in their talk in the hallways,

in the metaphors and language they use) that brings
the future powerfully into the present as a
mobilizing agent.[1]

Our future is an emergent reality created by our present
images of what we think it will be like. Our beliefs and
assumptions about what is acceptable, possible, desirable, and
meaningful influence the images we create. We can shift our
future by creating inspiring new images of what we want, and
then making small changes in the present that align with the
new images. As computer scientist Alan Kay said, "The best
way to predict the future is to invent it."

Positive Images Create Positive Futures

*If you want to build a ship, don't drum up the people
to gather wood, divide the work, and give orders.
Instead, teach them to yearn for the vast and
endless sea. ~Antoine de Saint Exupery*

We continuously form and hold images in our minds and then
live into those images. Images are a much more powerful
method for mobilizing change than concrete steps or
statements. Appreciative Inquiry (AI) suggests that some
images are more powerful than others in creating our futures.

Images are More Powerful than Abstract Ideas

Athletes have long known and practiced a form of future
imaging called visualization. The idea of visualization is to
picture something in your mind and make the experience as
real as possible. Senge writes how "world-class swimmers
have found that by imagining their hands to be twice their
actual size and their feet to be webbed, they actually swim
faster."[2] Golfer Jack Nicklaus describes how he uses images:

> I never hit a shot, even in practice, without having a
> very sharp, in-focus picture of it in my head. It's like
> a color movie. First I "see" the ball where I want it
> to finish, nice and white and sitting up high on the
> brightest green grass. Then the scene quickly
> changes and I "see" the ball going there: it's path,
> trajectory, and shape, even its behavior on landing.
> Then there's a sort of fade-out, and the next scene
> shows me the kind of swing that will turn the
> previous images into reality.[3]

Consultant and composer Robert Fritz describes how even simple images give "shape, contour, design, function, impression, feel, and life to what they describe."[4] He suggests we learn to form pictures of whatever we want in order to help make it happen. Cooperrider summarizes the work of various scholars describing the power of images over abstract ideas:

> …the underlying images held by a civilization or
> culture have an enormous influence on its fate.
> Ethical values such as "good" or "bad" have little
> force, except on an abstract level, but if those values
> emerge in the form of an image (for example, good
> = St. George, or bad = the Dragon), they suddenly
> become a power shaping the consciousness of
> masses of people.[5]

Images of the future are rich with possibilities for what might be. As we discuss possible scenarios for an upcoming wedding for example, we weave the future in our discourse. We discuss and create mental pictures and stories of how we think it will look, who will do what, and how it will play out. These images and stories affect our thinking and decisions that lead up to the event.

If we have a strong image of Uncle George drinking too much at our wedding, we might decide to hold the reception next to the hotel so people can walk to their rooms. If we create a stronger image around the flowers, decorations, and how everything will look, we might instead select a hotel and reception area that are more beautiful, but far away from each other. The decisions we make and the actions we take will be affected by images we hold. These decisions and actions create our future. The more powerful the image, the more it will drive our decisions, and the more likely it will come to pass.

All this speaks to the power of our collective images in creating reality. If we want a certain outcome, or desire change in an area of our lives, one of the most powerful things we can do is create a collective, inspiring, positive image of what we want. This will be much more effective than, say, making a list of the future items or changes we desire in our lives.

As we've touched on before, we can only create images of what we want and not what we don't want. For example, when we try to create an image of "no more war," there is an element of or reference to war somewhere in our image. Since we are creating a mental picture of "not" something, we tend to create unfocused, careless images of what will be in its place. We need to create deliberate images of what peace looks and feels like, and have conversations that build as clear and compelling a picture as we can about what we really want. Then we are creating images intentionally and deliberately.

The Wish Question

The classic positive question in AI for creating ideal future images is the "wish" question. It basically asks us to describe three wishes for the future within some context, such as our organization or relationship. The process of forming questions discussed in the previous chapter is useful in creating wish questions. The essential purpose is to create an ideal image of what we want most going forward. The wish question is usually preceded by other questions that put us in a positive frame of mind. Follow-up questions may include asking people what they can do now to achieve this ideal, or imagining what they did to get to this new future.

Solution-focused therapists have a variety of ideal future questions, and the classic one is often referred to as the "miracle question." It was conceived by therapist Steve de Shazer as an extension of Milton Erickson's crystal ball technique.[6] The miracle question is basically like this: "Suppose that one night while you were asleep, a miracle occurred and your problem was solved. How would you know? What would be different?"[7]

The focus of this question is on creating an image of what life would be like without the problem. The focus of the discussion after the miracle question is often on providing as many details as possible of this ideal scenario. In effect, it is creating as "real" and detailed an image as possible of the desired future. Examples of follow-up questions might include, "Who will be the first to notice [the change]?" "What will he do or say?" "How will you respond?"[8]

This questioning process can be particularly useful within AI to help develop our images further. We can ask detailed questions about our ideal future, and create real-life scenarios to help bring in the emotional, aesthetic, and spiritual components we discussed earlier. We can ask such questions as, "What will we be doing differently when we've reached our vision? What will be the first sign that things are changing for the better?"[9] Thinking through specific future scenarios makes the future image come alive and helps us get even more clear and passionate about what we want.

Robert Fritz has another approach for creating images of what we want from his Technologies for Change® program. He suggests the first step is starting with nothing, a "blank canvas," and gradually creating a mental picture of what we want from there.[10] Once you have an initial image of what you want, he suggests:

> Look at your result from many angles in your
> imagination. Try adding new elements. Try taking
> out elements. Look at the image from inside,
> outside, above, below, close, and distant. As you
> practice changing frames of reference, you will get
> to know more and more about what you want to
> create.[11]

Fritz's suggestion for evaluating our images from a variety of perspectives helps us get clear about what we really want. It brings the image to life.

Appreciative Inquiry basically takes Robert Fritz's idea one step further, in suggesting that we "weight" our thinking ahead of time by being in a positive frame of mind. In this sense our slate is not really blank, but contains positive feelings and possibly even images as we create. As we know from the Constructionist Principle, there really is no such thing as a neutral or objective state. Given this assumption, AI suggests we weight creative thinking in favor of the positive.

Positive Momentum

We can use questions within AI to move us into a positive state for creating images. We ask about things like high points, peak experiences, strengths, values, and so on. These questions create "positive momentum" from which we launch into the wish question.

There are other ways to create positive momentum in addition to questions. If we are alone we can use our favorite music, inspiring visual images, delicious food, a warm bath, or whatever makes us feel good. From this positive feeling we are best prepared to think about and have conversations about what we want in the future.

Future imaging, or visualization, can be done on an informal, day-to-day basis in terms of visualizing what we want for that day, that meeting, etc. It can also be done using a more in-depth formal process with an interview protocol. Creating positive images of what we want is something that can be learned with discipline and practice.[12] The more we practice, the better we become.

The Power of Vision

Few, if any, forces in human affairs are as powerful as shared vision. ~Peter Senge[13]

Some images or visions are more powerful than others. The more provocative, illuminating, and promising the future image, the more likely we are to move towards it.[14] In this section we consider different theories about what makes some images more powerful than others, and the nature of their inherent attractive force.

Creating Powerful Images

Sociologist Fred Polak did a study on future images in Western civilization that is often cited in AI material. He notes, "The rise and fall of images of the future precedes or accompanies the rise and fall of cultures."[15] He claims these images are the single most important predictor of what is ahead. We can simply listen to what people are saying about the future in any culture. If it is positive then things are going well; if not, the culture is in decline.

Polak points out that the cognitive part of these images is less of a factor than the emotional, esthetic, and spiritual aspects.[16] This suggests that our feelings about an image are just as important, or even more so, than the mental details. The more positive and intense our feelings about a future image, the stronger its ability to emerge. This is why AI questions about what we want are stated in such a provocative, compelling manner. The intent is to connect the most intensely positive, powerful feelings we can to the future image we desire.

Polak also talks about the esthetic and spiritual aspects of the future image as powerful forces. This domain exists as a recognized but relatively less explored resource within AI. The more pleasing or spiritually significant an image is to us, the more power it has as a constructive force in our lives. Sensorial aspects may include such things as beautiful art, pleasing music, wonderful smells, luscious food, comfortable chairs, or anything that arouses our sense in a pleasurable way.

Spiritually significant aspects are a bit more abstract, and include beliefs about why we are here, our deeper purpose, the meaning of life, and so on. One of the ways to get to this level of thinking is to continue asking what we really want and why. We keep asking these questions until we get to the deepest, most meaningful, or most profound level we can access. Creativity and personal mastery teacher Srikumar Rao suggests we ask such questions as, "Why is it you want to do what you do?" "How is it a reflection of your values?" "How does it relate to your unique purpose in life?" "What is it that you want to accomplish in society?"[17]

David Cooperrider and Marge Schiller helped a client get to a deeper level in one of the classic AI cases with Avon Mexico.[18] Cooperrider asked Rita from Avon what she wanted to learn about and achieve with the intervention. Rita responded that they wanted "to dramatically cut the incidence of sexual harassment." Cooperrider then said, "O.K. Rita... But is that all?" This question took Rita into that deeper place of imaging we are trying to describe. Rita replied, "You mean what do I *really* want to see?" She paused, and then responded: "What we really want to see is the development of the new century organization—a model of high quality cross-gender relationships in the workplace." Rita went to a grander, more inspiring image when she answered from that deeper, more creative and meaningful place. The organization went on to achieve this vision, receiving the *Catalyst Award for best place in the country for women to work.*[19]

Vision as a Field

There are several interesting conceptual notions of the attractive force of vision or future image. Vision has traditionally been thought of in linear terms as a destination of sorts. Today we are here, and tomorrow we hope to be there. The vision acts like a linear force, pulling us like a stretched rubber-band to the future image. Fritz describes this force as "structural tension."[20] He suggests there are several factors that influence the strength of this force, including the strength and clarity of the future image as well as the size of the gap between where we are and what we want.

Margaret Wheatley proposes another metaphor for vision in *Leadership and the New Science.* She suggests we consider it as a field:

> In linear fashion we have most often conceived of vision as designing the future, creating a destination for the organization. We have believed that the clearer the image of the destination, the more force the future would exert on the present, pulling us to that desired state. It's a very strong Newtonian image, much like the old view of gravity. But what if we changed the science and looked at vision as a field?

> If vision is a field, think about what we could do differently to use its formative influence. We would start by recognizing that in creating a vision, we are creating a power, not a place, an influence, not a destination. This field metaphor would help us understand that we need congruency in the air, visionary messages matched by visionary behaviors.[21]

Wheatley is suggesting we can be more effective in creating what we want by attending to the "invisible influences" that support the vision, and realizing that vision is more of a guidance system than a location. The "force" of the vision still exists, but there are also "invisible influences" in the field. These influences might include such things as our conversations, cultural beliefs, values, and behaviors. We can become better creators by becoming more aware of these influences and trying to align them to our vision.

I see two relevant pieces in this field metaphor for AI. The first is the notion of attending to the field. The future image is still critical in creating what we want, but our daily behaviors, thoughts, actions, and conversations can either compete with or support our movement towards those images. Working it from both ends may help us achieve what we want more quickly. The second piece is in the concept of vision as a power rather than a place. This is a more difficult concept to articulate, and I believe it shows up in the addition of the emotional, aesthetic, and spiritual aspects of the vision described previously. The cognitive, descriptive image (what it looks like) seems to represent the Newtonian "location" aspect of the vision. The emotional, aesthetic, and spiritual aspects (what it feels like, what it really means to us) might be the other factors that make up the power of the visionary field. Attending to both realms will increase the power. The future vision is not just a place we are heading to in isolation; it also includes certain feelings and deeper meanings we desire in general and in our relationship with others.

The essential idea is that our images are possibly deeper and broader than some of the current thinking would suggest. Our images not only provide beacons of direction, but perhaps actually help attract congruent thoughts, people, etc. It's not too far of a stretch to consider the possibility that formative fields help create some of the miraculous "coincidences" that often emerge with strong visions.

Practical Considerations

We can become aware of our future images of even mundane activities, such as going to the grocery store, and realize their formative influence. We can do a scaled-down version of the visualization techniques used by athletes for our daily activities. Some people refer to this as setting intentions, and I have found it to be extremely helpful.

I begin each morning by listing the major activities for the day. I then spend a brief moment on each activity, imagining what I want unfolding in my mind. If I have something particularly big going on, I spend extra time visualizing the event. Positive emotion is critical in this exercise as we described earlier, or else it has minimal effect. I have found that my success rate is much higher with this practice than without it, and it is now a regular part of my day.

Daily visioning, or intention setting also seems to work because it helps me get clear about what I really want in the situation. It helps me rise above my impulses or short term wants in the moment to remember the bigger picture and my greater aspirations. Clarity helps me stay centered and focused on the right things, and facilitates any decision-making I have to do. This in turn helps create the experience I desire.

There is no denying the power of images to manifest what we want, whatever the dynamics involved. Images are gratuitously provided by our friends, family, the media, and others unless we become intentional about creating them ourselves. To create the life we want, we must be intentional about creating images of what we want. The more provocative, meaningful, and inspiring our vision is, the more power it has in our lives.

Vision Before Decision

*Most people fail instead of succeeding because they
trade what they want most for what they want
in the moment. ~Jack Graff*

Our lives are a product of our cumulative decisions, which are
guided by our beliefs and images about the future. If we decide
and act in response to an image of what we want at the highest
level, our actions will lead us to that future ideal. Cooperrider
suggests that one of the most important things we can do to
achieve a better future is to create a positive image of that
future.[22]

Vision Aligns Decisions

If we do not intentionally create future images, we are again
operating from the automatic images of our friends, families,
and culture. Debbie Ford explains:

> In any given moment we are being guided by one of
> two maps: a vision map, which is a deliberate plan
> for our future, or a default map, which is made up of
> our past. Choices made from our default map–our
> repetitive, automatic programming—do not nourish
> our flames, nor do they move us closer to our
> dreams. And even though they may feel right to us,
> they do so simply because they are familiar.[23]

She uses the term *conscious choices* to describe decisions made
in alignment with our vision. This means reflecting on the
effect of our choices on our future and our lives as a whole.[24]

In her book, *The Right Questions*, Ford provides a series of
questions to ask prior to making a decision in order to assure it
is in our best interest. It includes such things as, "Will this
choice propel me toward an inspiring future or will it keep me

stuck in the past? Will this choice bring me long-term fulfillment or will it bring me short-term gratification?"[25] In order to answer these questions, we must first know what we want. If we do not create a deliberate vision or ideal image of the future, our choices will not be clear. Stephen Covey writes that the "Second habit of highly effective people" is to "Begin with the end in mind."[26] It basically suggests that we need to have an overall vision or guiding image of what we want, and then align our daily decisions and actions to that vision. The stronger the image and the more emotion we have around it, the more likely we are to act in accordance with it.

For example, if you just had a heart attack one week ago, and the doctor tells you to lose weight to stay alive, your chance of acting on this survival image is pretty high. The next day it will be relatively clear and easy for you to choose the gym over the doughnut store. On the other hand, if you arbitrarily decide one day that it would be nice to lose a few pounds, this relatively weaker vision with little emotion will make the same decision much less clear. Your competing image of the tasty doughnut will likely exert a stronger emotional force than the gym.

Clarity Helps Answers "Pop"

Robert Fritz also underscores the importance of choice aligning with vision. He describes how making decisions is a learned ability, and we can become better with practice.[27] Becoming clear about what we want improves our decision-making capability, which causes what we want to "pop" out of the seemingly infinite chaos of possibilities. In this age of complexity, this is a very intriguing notion.

In other words, if we become clear that we want more beauty in our lives, beautiful things begin to show up where none seemed to exist before. All of a sudden we notice art galleries along roads we have driven for years. We begin to notice how attractive our friends are in ways we never saw before. It's like we create new choices that contain more of what we want. Life experience is rich, and we can find whatever we want in a situation or person. Our attention to something makes it grow larger.

Fritz provides a practical example of how knowing what we want facilitates decision-making. In the following excerpt he compares how he has learned to choose from a restaurant menu as compared to his friend who has not:

> I would open the menu and quickly select an item. During the first experimental stage, I was sometimes delighted, sometimes disappointed. Over time I learned to let my eyes be drawn to just the right items and to make my choice immediately. After the choice was made, I would study the menu and check out the decision. I was almost always right. Somehow *I had learned to be quickly drawn directly to what I wanted* [italics added] and to order it with confidence that I would enjoy the result of my choice.
>
> I asked my friend how he made his choice.
>
> He told me he carefully studied each offering and compared every one with every other one. If the menu offered many choices, he had quite a job. He had to read everything in the menu to make sure he did not miss something he might want.
>
> As we talked, he noticed that this was a common way he made many other choices in his life. *Rather than looking directly for what he wanted, he weighed all the available options* [italics added].[28]

This is a powerful tool for change in today's complex world. Information overload is a common notion, and one way to sort through it is to get clear about what we want. This helps what we want emerge before us, rather than looking through everything to find it. People sometimes complain that there are too many choices in today's world, but the heart of the issue may be that they are not clear about what they really want.

Fritz explains that choice is a developed ability that takes practice.[29] He provides examples of how we can learn to choose in his book, *The Path of Least Resistance*. He explains how "after you practice making choices, you begin to develop an instinct for making the *right* choices, the ones that lead to the most successful realization of what you want to create."[30] This book also offers a nice overview of the creative process and how we can become more effective in generating what we want.

We Conceive What We Believe

Whether you think you can, or you think you can't, either way you're right. ~Henry Ford

The images we construct of the future are consistent with our current beliefs and experiences about the future. They both work together in creating our reality, and it's sort of a chicken-and-egg scenario. Our current beliefs and assumptions define our thinking around what is possible, likely, and desired in the future, which create our future images. Our future images then act like beacons directing our current behavior and actions, and simultaneously re-constructing those very same beliefs from which they were formed.

Images Guide Automatic Thinking

All day long we act in accordance to images and beliefs we have about the future. This is another aspect to our automatic thinking that wonderfully manages our lives. For example, right now you have decided to read this book. This decision was based in part from a belief of what you think the future will hold. Suppose you just discovered that an earthquake is predicted to hit your vicinity within the next 24 hours. Your decision to continue reading this book will be affected by this different future image.

Your current beliefs about earthquakes along with this one in particular will influence the future image you construct and the action you take. If you believe this will be a minor tremor, you might just continue reading and not alter much more in your life. If you are terrified of earthquakes, or believe this one could impact you significantly, you would probably put this book down and attend to other areas of your life.

Our present thinking and actions respond to our future images, and so do our bodies. As we hear the news of an impending earthquake, physical changes take place. If it is particularly threatening, we may enter a "fight or flight" state where our heart rate increases and adrenaline surges, along with a number of other physical changes. There have been numerous studies done which demonstrate that physical changes occur in response to our thoughts and images.

Images are Formed in Conversations

We continuously construct and act from our beliefs about the future in our conversations with ourselves and others. We discuss what we will do later, what kind of relationship we want to have, who we will have to dinner on Saturday. These discussions are rich with possibility. As we discussed in the Poetic Principle, whatever we focus on grows. If we continue to talk about how scared we are about an upcoming job interview, our experience of fear in that situation will escalate. If we imagine and discuss ways to be more relaxed, we will create a more relaxing experience.

Conversations with others are a powerful way to work intentionally with our future images. First, it is easier to look at our spoken words than our thoughts, so conversations provide more tangible or obvious insight about our images. Second, they occur regularly throughout the day, so we have continuous opportunity to re-create images we desire. Finally, they offer a direct and powerful form of co-construction. We can integrate other ideas and perspectives in a more direct and relevant manner than from the "voices" in our heads.

As we become more aware of the power of our conversations, we realize that each one is either moving us closer to or further from what we want. Learning to have more deliberate conversations that continually build greater possibilities for the future is a skill worth developing. The first step is to become more aware of whether we are speaking positively or negatively about future events. If we are speaking positively, then we know we are creating more of what we want. We can continue to build on the positive aspects to enhance the image even further. If we are thinking or speaking negatively about some image of the future, we can intentionally shift our conversations to create a more positive version. If we become more aware of our conversations, we'll become more effective in creating images that reflect what we truly want in our lives.

If we are not aware in our conversations, we automatically take on the future images provided to us by default in our relationships, culture, families, etc. We take up professions that please our parents, dress in ways that fit our culture, and bathe regularly like everyone else. We are infused with images from the media about what we should do, be, and look like. If we act with awareness, we can be more intentional about which aspects we adopt.

Beliefs Channel Images

This process of automatically adopting the cultural beliefs around us is another aspect of our miraculous automatic thinking. It serves important functions in helping us live together by providing similar mental frameworks so we can collectively make sense of the world. It helps us get along and organize in ways that sustain life. Appreciative Inquiry suggests we can leverage this gift further by becoming more aware of what we are taking in. We may still decide to do the same things or think the same way when we become more aware, but our action is now deliberate and we feel more confident in this area.

One of the unconscious ideas we learn from the world around us is what is possible. The prevailing beliefs and norms of our culture and families and educational institutions tell us what is and is not achievable. As discussed earlier, our beliefs about what is possible create some of our greatest barriers. Cooperrider states that, "the greatest obstacle in the way of group and organizational well-being is the positive image, the affirmative projection that guides the group or the organization."[31]

There are numerous examples of how beliefs about what is possible define behavior. No one was ever able to run a mile in less than four minutes, but once Roger Bannister accomplished this amazing feat others immediately followed. There are some who suggest that the only limitations we have are our beliefs.[32] It is difficult for us to break the barrier of what we think is possible. As author Ralph Charell said, "Nobody exceeds beyond his or her wildest expectations, unless he or she begins with some wild expectations."

I recently asked a friend what he hoped for in the future. He said that he thought being happy about 30% of the time was about as good as one could expect. In that moment I really understood the limitations of our positive beliefs for the first time. I was shocked at how low his expectations were, and realized mine used to be about the same several years ago. It is always easier to see things in other people, and I could see how this limiting belief was influencing all that he did. There was no desire for him to change to a more satisfying job, or do anything in his life that would add to his happiness as long as he was hitting that 30% mark. I could easily see how his underlying belief of how happy one can reasonably be smothered his desire for more, and kept him complacent in a life well below what was possible.

What do you believe is possible? How happy do you think a person can reasonably expect to be? The answers to these questions are your personal happiness limits. Consider where these beliefs come from, and what would happen if you pushed the envelope a bit. The more you work with the principles in this book, the greater your ability to create a life you want and the happier you will become. The happier and more successful you become, the easier it will be for you to expand your beliefs about what is possible. Positive experience and provocative images are two of the best ways to shift limiting beliefs. As Kenny Rogers said, "Don't be afraid to give up the good for the great."

Big Change Begins Small

Never doubt that a small group of committed citizens can change the world. Indeed, it's the only thing that ever has. ~Margaret Mead

Webster's dictionary defines change as "the exchange of one thing for another; a new occupation or fresh outlook; the passing from one form, phase, place, or state to another.[33] When we think of change, often we think of a concrete event, or an observable difference. We think of buying a new car or getting married as a change. What we often fail to recognize is that what we perceive as "a change" is actually a culmination of many smaller and ongoing changes that collectively led up to the point we believe change occurred.

Change is Continuous

Consider the many things that happen prior to the change of getting married. We meet our spouse and have numerous conversations and experiences that continuously and incrementally shift our thoughts about this person and our relationship. Conversations and experiences with others about the person and about marriage influence our thinking as well. Each one of these incremental activities contributes in some way to the ultimate decision and action.

A small difference in any of these incremental experiences can affect the ultimate change. For example, one conversation with an influential person might alter our decision about having the same last names. We might shift our attire decisions after observing a picture of the latest bridal fashions as we walk past a newsstand. A bad bachelor party experience might end the whole thing or shift the experience significantly. Each incremental experience contributes to the ultimate change in some way.

Different people will experience or recognize change at different points. In a more traditional setting, the husband might experience change as he walks out of the church with his new wife on his arm. It might occur for the woman as she accepts his engagement proposal and puts the ring on her finger. The church deems it official once vows are exchanged, and the government recognizes it upon filing appropriate documents.

The essential idea is that change is ongoing and not just one moment in time. We think of it as the concrete perceivable event, but in reality it is occurring continuously. Our incremental experiences and conversations imperceptibly change our thoughts, beliefs, images, and actions, which eventually lead up to perceivable changes. The action and perceived change of getting married was prefaced by a host of incremental decisions and shifts in beliefs that moved us towards the ultimate change.

Our bodies are continuously changing along with our thoughts. Barry Kaufman describes how our bodies undergo constant change and regeneration:

Ninety-eight percent of the atoms of our bodies are replaced in the course of a year. Our skeleton, which appears so fundamentally stable and solid, undergoes an almost complete transition every three months. Our skin regenerates within four weeks, our stomach lining within four days and the portion of our stomach lining which interfaces with food reconstructs itself every four or five minutes.[34]

He goes on to explain how the universe and earth are in a constant state of flux as well. He suggests we learn to flow with the never-ending dance of change rather than trying to hold on to fixed ways of thinking and being.

We need to think in terms of change as the norm, with the seemingly stable periods in between as simply incremental movements we can't yet perceive. As we discussed in the Constructionist Principle, the relatively insignificant events in each day are what really constitute our lives. As American Congressman Bruce Barton wrote, "Sometimes when I consider what tremendous consequences come from little things... I am tempted to think...there are no little things."

An Example of Incremental Change

Here is another example of how continuous change works. Suppose we are out to dinner with a friend and have a brief discussion about how clean and well-cared-for the restaurant appears to be. The next day, we catch a television program that talks about ways to clean more efficiently. A week later, we come home from work and notice a layer of dust on the furniture. Upon seeing the dust, and being influenced by recent experiences, we make a decision to clean a bit more often using one of the ideas we saw on television.

This small change in cleaning over time leads us to feel a bit better about ourselves, and builds up just enough confidence to try a new class that looks interesting. Positive feedback from our teacher in the class leads us to take more classes.

Additional positive reinforcement from the new classes leads us to take a few more, and ultimately get a degree. Our new degree leads to a career change and promising new job.

As we go about our life in this example, the only pieces we might think of as changes are in cleaning habits, taking classes, and the new job. Change was actually continually occurring the entire time. Our confidence was incrementally being built with each small experience. Class discussions, support from friends, homework experiences, interactions with strangers, grades, and a myriad of other influences all contributed to the "big" career change. A shift in any one of these small areas, such as experiencing a demoralizing teacher in the first class, could have altered the course of events.

Small Changes Build

This story also illustrates a concept called a reinforcing loop[35] or amplifying feedback loop.[36] Psychologist Milton Erickson described this as the snowball effect[37] and noted by Cooperrider earlier, Carl Weick described something similar with "small wins."[38] In these types of experiences, one positive incident builds upon another, creating a momentum which leads to a significant perceivable change. This process can also work in reverse, creating negative loops or spirals.

Marla Cilley, also known as the "Fly Lady," is well aware of this small change concept. She moved herself out of serious depression by starting ever so slowly in cleaning up her house. In her book, "Sink Reflections"[39] and through her free website,[40] she helps women (and men) slowly build their confidence by starting small and creating positive spirals. She begins by having them clean the kitchen sink, and then slowly adding other cleaning practices as personal satisfaction and confidence build. She has helped countless people "FLY" (**F**irst **L**ove **Y**ourself) with this approach, and it all begins with the small act of cleaning a sink.

Therapists O'Hanlon and Weiner-Davis explain how "once a small positive change is made, people feel optimistic and a bit more confident about tackling further changes."[41] Peter Senge describes how "small changes can produce big results—but the areas of highest leverage are often the least obvious."[42] Wheatley and Kellner-Rogers explain how this works in community-organizing efforts:

> People work on a small effort and discover new skills. Their energy and belief in themselves grow; they take on another project, then another. Looking back, they see that they have created a larger system whose capacities were undreamed of when they first began.[43]

The essential idea is that big changes don't have to be tackled with big plans or major overhauls. We can find some small way to begin moving in the direction of our desires, and let positive spiraling work in our favor.

Without going into depth on chaos theory, Wheatley suggests that meaning is the "strange attractor" in human systems change.[44] In other words, the small changes that have the biggest potential to impact and organize our lives are the ones that are most meaningful to us. What is meaningful will be different for each person, and will change continuously. What is meaningful in the moment is strongly influenced by the images we have of the future. Again, we come full circle. We might choose to browse through the real-estate section of the newspaper if we are thinking about selling our home. If we are not planning on moving anywhere, we might skip this section and read another section that is more relevant or meaningful to us. Our images and beliefs about what is meaningful guide our actions.

Changes occur within this incremental approach so slowly that often they are imperceptible from day-to-day. It is like watching a puppy grow up. You don't see any difference from one day to the next, and then one weekend you realize his collar is too tight.

Benefits of Incremental Change

There are five benefits in using this incremental, emergent change approach to create what we want. They are:

1) It allows our underlying beliefs to slowly shift along with us. We are often not aware of all the beliefs that sustain a current pattern of thinking or behavior. By introducing change slowly, conflicts in beliefs and thinking habits will surface in a manageable way.

2) It gives our relationships a chance to grow with us. The more gradual the change, the less likely people are to notice or resist it. They gradually shift right along with us.

3) It allows our support systems to gradually change along with us. This helps to sustain and reinforce the new behaviors. Examples of support systems include our financial system, eating regimes, work places, schools, and government and community institutions.

4) The changes are relatively easy to make since the new behaviors and actions are fairly close to our existing ones. Sudden, bigger changes are often hard to sustain, because our underlying beliefs are still reflective of our old ways of being and tend to pull us back.

5) It allows us to experiment and play with our emerging reality and adjust our vision accordingly. If we can be open to the changes emerging in the present, we can find ways to weave them into our future desires.

We live in a continuously evolving world where the future is less certain and cause and effect relationships are not as clear. We need to shift our emphasis to be more in the present moment and work with what is appearing. This means we need to learn to make small, continuous changes now to realize our dreams. Wheatley and Kellner-Rogers describe it like this:

> An emergent world asks us to stand in a different place. We can no longer stand at the end of something we visualize in detail and plan backwards from that future. Instead, we must stand at the beginning, clear in our intent, with a willingness to be involved in discovery. The world asks that we focus less on how we can coerce something to make it conform to our designs and focus more on how we can engage with one another, how we can enter into the experience and then notice what comes forth. It asks that we participate more than plan.[45]

This suggests we flow more with life, expecting and embracing the inevitable "surprises" that emerge from the "invisible influences." While this sounds like a bad Star Wars® movie, it essentially means we need to be more open to what life presents. By flowing with life and applying positive incremental changes over time, momentum begins to build and one day we wake up and realize we are simply living the vision we have aspired to.

It all begins with a compelling image of the future. We can then look for some small way in our lives to begin moving towards that future. This movement does not have to be an action. It can be shifting our conversations, questions, or focus to pay more attention to what we want. We have described ways to make these small shifts throughout the book, and will continue in the next chapters.

Final Thoughts

Our collective images or visions of the future create that future. The more positive, provocative, and compelling the image, the greater its force in manifesting. Our co-constructed beliefs about what is possible, probable, and desirable strongly influence the images we construct. We continuously construct images of the future in our conversations with ourselves and others, and we take control of our lives when we become more aware and deliberate about the images we construct.

Clear images help guide us in daily decision-making and action. Small positive changes towards the desired future spiral into large, sustainable changes over time. These changes don't have to be actions; they can be as simple as choosing to notice or ask about what we want more of in our lives.

As Lewis Caroll said, "If you do not know where you're going, any road will take you there." Even better is Yogi Berra's advice that, "If you don't know where you are going, you'll end up some place else."

CHAPTER 5

The Positive Principle

When we seek to discover the best
in others, we somehow bring out the
best in ourselves.

~ WILLIAM ARTHUR WARD

The Positive Principle states, "Momentum for change requires large amounts of positive affect and social bonding—things like hope, excitement, inspiration, caring, camaraderie, sense of urgent purpose, and sheer joy in creating something meaningful together."[1] This principle suggests that positive emotion is essential for growth and optimal functioning. It creates energy and momentum for change, and provides important resources for short and long-term physical and mental health.

It's Good to Feel Good[2]

Happiness does not depend on outward things, but
on the way we see them. ~Leo Tolstoy

There is a lot more to feeling good than the fleeting experience of positive emotion. Positive Psychology research shows that positive feelings have a much larger role in cognitive functioning, health and well-being than we previously thought. Professor Barbara Fredrickson of the University of Michigan has done significant research on positive emotion and has created a framework she calls the *broaden-and-build theory*:

> This theory states that certain discrete positive emotions—including joy, interest, contentment, pride, and love—although phenomenologically distinct, all share the ability to broaden people's momentary thought-action repertoires and build their enduring personal resources, ranging from physical and intellectual resources to social and psychological resources.[3]

She suggests that positive emotions are not simply pleasant, fleeting experiences, but play important roles that are essential to healthy life. They broaden thinking and build physical, social, intellectual, and psychological resources that develop personal strength, resilience, and wellness.[4]

Positive Emotions Broaden Thinking and Actions

There are four main propositions in the *broaden-and-build* framework. The first is "Positive emotions broaden the scope of attention and thought-action repertoires."[5] Previous emotion studies focused primarily on "action urges" produced by negative emotion, such as flight in fear, or attack in anger. These responses represent a narrowing of what Fredrickson calls thought-action repertoires. In other words, our choices about what to do or think become very limited as we experience fear, anger, grief, etc. Our survival instinct kicks in to dictate our thoughts and actions in a narrow set of ways that protect us.

Fredrickson suggests that positive emotions expand or broaden our options for what to do and think since they do not produce the limiting survival responses. Her research shows that if we feel good, our cognitive functioning is better and so is our attention. Our thinking becomes more expansive, and we are able to create a much wider repertoire of possibilities for thought and action. When we feel good we are more helpful[6] and are more inclusive of others. Fredrickson cites the work of Isen and colleagues which shows that people experiencing positive affect are also more flexible, creative, integrative, open to information, and efficient.[7]

Fredrickson completed one particularly interesting study on the effect of positive emotion and own-race bias (ORB) in face recognition. ORB is a well-known psychological phenomenon where we have difficulty distinguishing differences in the faces of people from other races. She cites the colloquial phrase, "They all look alike to me."

One study was previously done that showed intensive training reduced the effect of ORB for a short time, but the effect was gone within a week.[8] Fredrickson was able to eliminate the effect of ORB in her study by inducing states of joy and humor into test participants.[9] In other words, when having a good time, people recognize and distinguish faces from other races as easily as they do those from their own race. This is a great example of just one of the many ways that positive emotion can broaden cognitive ability.

The implications of the *broaden-and-build* hypothesis are extensive. The framework suggests that boardrooms and work places would be more productive and effective if people were enjoying themselves. It implies that we will be more successful in dealing with personal conflict when we feel good than in the heat of the moment. It suggests that leaders will make better decisions if they are content or having fun. It hints at the possibility of looking at our learning environments, and attending to the feelings of the teachers and students in consideration of learning effectiveness. It builds a strong case for feeling good anytime we need to work together or be productive. The possibilities are intriguing.

Positive Emotions Undo Negative Ones

The second proposition in the framework is "Positive emotions undo lingering negative emotions."[10] Her research shows that heart rates and other cardiovascular measurements return to normal more quickly when people experience positive emotion after a stressful situation. She found that even mild positive feelings such as contentment help undo the effects of difficult experiences. She explains that the reasons positive emotions work effectively to counteract negative emotions is that they broaden our thinking to allow for more productive and fruitful options. She explains:

> It may be that building empathy between people and groups works to reduce prejudice, aggression, and violence, because it taps into the broadening effects of love and builds social alliances and bonds. Likewise, invoking music and laughter, may work to de-escalate anger and interpersonal conflict as well as to combat stress and illness because it taps into the broadening effects of joy and builds social bonds and coping resources. Experiences of flow and intrinsic motivation may similarly work to improve the quality of life and foster psychological development because they tap into the broadening effects of interest, and build intellectual resources.[11]

I find it interesting in Fredrickson's research that positive emotions don't necessarily have to be related to the negative event in order to work. In other words, if we have a disagreement with our friend, we don't need to find ways to necessarily feel better about her or the situation. We can go for a swim, read the comics, or do some other unrelated activity that makes us feel good in order to reverse the lingering effects of the disagreement.

Positive Emotions Build Resiliency

Fredrickson's third assumption is "Positive emotions fuel psychological resiliency."[12] Psychological resilience is defined as being able to bounce back quickly and efficiently from stressful experiences. Her research shows that positive emotions are a critical component in resilience and help buffer people from depression. In a study of the effects of the US terrorist attacks on September 11, 2001, she found more resilient people experienced a higher degree of positive feelings during and after the crisis than their less-resilient counterparts, and, in fact seemed to thrive.[13] They were also less likely to develop depression tendencies afterwards. It was interesting to note that people experience positive emotions even during a crisis, such as feelings of gratitude for being safe, or feeling closer to loved ones.

Fredrickson suggests that one of the best ways to cultivate positive emotions, including during a crisis, is to find positive meaning in the situation.[14] She mentions a variety of possibilities, such as reframing events positively, finding the spiritual or philosophical meaning, employing relaxation techniques, or reflecting on good times. We've discussed a number of ways to do this in this book as well.

Therapist and author Barry Kaufman has an interesting proposition in his book, *Happiness is a Choice*.[15] He suggests that making happiness the priority in our lives is the best way to achieve consistent positive emotion. It's an intriguing and relatively simple idea that I have found to be very beneficial. He explains that most of what we want, such as certain careers, partners, experiences, or things is something we believe will ultimately make us happy. He suggests we "cut to the chase," and simply look for ways to be happy now. The interesting piece in this is that the things we want come more effectively and efficiently with this approach. It may be due to the broadening of thought-action repertoires which arise from simply feeling good more often.

Positive Emotions Create Upward Spirals

Fredrickson's final assumption in the *broaden-and-build* theory states, "Positive emotions build psychological resilience and fuel upward spirals toward improved emotional well-being."[16] This proposition suggests that the effects of positive emotions accumulate and compound over time, leading to optimal functioning and significant increases in well-being.[17] People are able to build capacity for dealing with future difficulties from the broadened thinking resulting from positive emotions in the present. Fredrickson explains:

> Positive emotions trigger upward spirals by broadening individuals' habitual modes of thinking and action and building lasting resources that promote future experiences of positive emotions. As this cycle continues, positive emotions transform individuals into more resilient, socially integrated, and capable versions of themselves. So, positive emotions not only make people feel good in the present, but they also increase the likelihood that people will function well and feel good in the future.[18]

Resilient people, who also had the highest levels of positive emotion, came out of the September 11, 2001 crisis stronger than they went in. "They emerged from their anguish more satisfied with life, more optimistic, and more tranquil—and likely more resilient—than before."[19]

Fredrickson also cites the work of Staw, Sutton, and Pellod which shows how positive emotions within organizational settings "can transform individuals into more creative, effective, socially integrated—and perhaps even better paid—workers."[20] The positive spiral within organizations is especially strong due to the contagious nature[21] of positive emotions.

Laughter

Norman Cousins is one of the most well-known people on the benefits of laughter. He is famous for having "laughed" himself out of a supposedly irreversible crippling disease.[22] He watched films of the Marx Brothers and Candid Camera during his illness, and was read a variety of humor books such as White's *Subtreasury of American Humor* and Max Eastman's *The Enjoyment of Laughter*. Early in his treatment he found that ten minutes of genuine belly laughter gave him at least two hours of pain free sleep.[23] He recovered from his supposedly irreversible illness through these positive emotions in conjunction with positive beliefs and large doses of Vitamin C.

An organization called Rx Laughter®, founded by network executive Sherry Hilber, is attempting to pick up where Cousins left off. Their ultimate vision is to create a comedy network in all hospital treatment areas. They have begun work with the UCLA School of Medicine, and have seed funding from Comedy Central. Preliminary results have shown that "children and adolescents who watch funny programs are able to withstand painful procedures longer, and with less overall anxiety."[24] They believe that humor benefits the patients as well as the families, and hope to learn more about how it may improve immune function and speed of healing.

Other Positive Emotion Research

John Gottman's research further supports the case for positive interactions. In 1990 he and his colleagues videotaped a fifteen minute conversation between each of 700 newly married couples. They calculated the ratio of positive to negative moments during the conversation, and made predictions based on the ratio of which couples would be married and divorced ten years later.[25] Their predictions turned out to be 94% accurate! The ratio used in the study from Gottman's years of previous research was 5 to 1.[26] In other words, couples experiencing at least five positive interactions for each negative one stayed together.

Dr. Seligman has completed and compiled extensive research on happiness, which he writes about in his book, *Authentic Happiness*. Here are but a few of his findings:

> Happy people... have better health habits, lower blood pressure, and feistier immune systems than less happy people.

> In the largest study to date, 2,282 Mexican-Americans from the southwest United Sates aged sixty-five or older were given a battery of demographic and emotional tests, then tracked for two years. Positive emotion strongly predicted who lived and who died, as well as disability...the researchers found that happy people were half as likely to die, and half as likely to become disabled.

> Happier people are markedly more satisfied with their jobs than less happy people, ...[and] more happiness actually causes more productivity and higher income.

> Adults and children who are put into a good mood select higher goals, perform better, and persist longer on a variety of laboratory tasks, such as solving anagrams.

> Children and adults who are made happy display more empathy and are willing to donate more money to others in need.

> "Very happy" people differed markedly from
> average people and from unhappy people in one
> principal way: a rich and fulfilling social life.[27]

The case for feeling good is strong. When experiencing positive emotion we are more creative, attentive, flexible, open-minded, helpful, empathetic, generous, effective, efficient, productive, resilient, healthy, socially well-adjusted, and well-paid. Oh, and we also feel good. Optimal health and functioning are not created by simply reducing or eliminating negative emotions and affects, but by building positive ones. It is definitely good to feel good.[28]

The Positive Core

People travel to wonder at the height of the mountains,
at the huge waves of the seas,...and yet they pass by
themselves without wondering. ~St. Augustine

One of the most popular ways within AI to build positive emotion is to inquire into something called the "positive core." The positive core is defined by Cooperrider and Whitney as the "wisdom, knowledge, successful strategies, positive attitudes and affect, best practices, skills, resources, and capabilities of the organization."[29] It is what the organization does best, is most proud of, and positively identifies with.

On a personal level, the positive core is comprised of the same qualities. It contains our wisdom, knowledge, successful life strategies, positive attitudes, strengths, skills, aspirations, resources, and capabilities, and is present in all people and situations. Everyone and every situation has a positive core. Think of someone that you don't particularly like, and consider that this person has the following:

>Achievements, assets, unexplored potentials,
>innovations, strengths, elevated thoughts,
>opportunities, high point moments, traditions,
>competencies, stories, expressions of wisdom,
>insights into their deeper spirit or soul, and visions
>of valued and possible futures.[30]

This positive core is a dynamic concept that is in constant
motion. It is a construction like everything else we perceive,
open to infinite interpretations. It continuously evolves and
changes along with us, new in every moment.

Focusing on the Positive Core

As we focus on the positive core it transforms and strengthens
as it is noticed and affirmed.[31] What we focus on grows, and
the process of simply looking for those positive attributes
strengthens and augments that inner core. Focusing on our
greatest attributes makes those attributes come alive, becoming
stronger and more present through our attention to them.

Asking about the positive core is an essential tool in
organizational development work to draw out and unleash the
positive potential within the organization. The same is true in
our personal lives. We can unleash our potential for greatness
as we ask questions about, and focus on our positive core. We
can also do this with other people and our life experiences.
Finding what is good at the heart of a person or situation is a
powerful way to build enthusiasm, momentum, and energy for
personal change and growth.

One of the most transforming exercises I have done is to
write about the positive core of each of my children, my
husband, and myself. I took approximately five minutes per
person, depending on how much time I had, and listed every
positive aspect I could find about them. I did this roughly every
other day, and I could write a separate chapter on how it
transformed our relationships. It also caused me to notice more

positive aspects in others. Suffice it to say that focusing on the best of others truly draws it out.

As I discussed in previous chapters, we have a choice about what we pay attention to. It takes deliberate effort to focus on the positive core if we have been conditioned to notice the negative. A critical, problem-focused culture influences us to think about people and situations in a critical, problem-focused manner. When we actively try to look for the good it can feel uncomfortable or different from our typical way of critically viewing people. If we continue to look for the good we will change our habituated way of seeing others so we automatically begin to notice the positive core attributes.

For example, at first we might feel angry towards a check-out clerk who is cold and unfriendly and then realize we are focusing on the negative. Negative feelings such as anger and frustration can act as a barometer to let us know when we are focused on something we don't want. Once we realize we are not focusing on what we want, we can make a deliberate choice to shift and look for "the offender's" positive core. We might then notice that he is also fast and efficient. Eventually we'll form an automatic habit of seeing the good things automatically, with less emphasis on the negative, but it will take practice. We may need to work a little harder at finding the good things if our initial experience was especially negative, but the good things are always there. As we focus on those positive core areas we bring them to life.

Eyeglass Story

I had one experience with this while getting eyeglasses during a special one-day sale. I arrived to a store filled with people. Normally I would have walked out, but I needed these glasses as soon as possible. I waited patiently for one hour for my turn. I found the woman who finally worked with me to be rude and inconsiderate of the time I had just spent waiting. We spent a frustrating few minutes deliberating my eyeglass selection, and

I could feel my anger building by the minute. Then I realized I was feeling negatively towards her, and knew this was not going to help the situation. I made a deliberate choice to shift my thinking and it took every ounce of strength I had.

I focused on the fact that others kept coming to her for questions, so she must know what she's doing. I decided to tell her, and although I couldn't perceive any change in her attitude after I told her, I noticed it made me feel a little better. We continued to debate eyeglasses and I struggled for another positive. I considered the craziness of this place and realized you couldn't pay me enough to work under these conditions. I began to admire how hard she was working, and realized she had probably been going at this pace for hours. I told her so. She responded by commenting on how she had worked through lunch and had not had a break since she started that morning. I still could not see much change in her attitude, but I was really beginning to admire her stamina and dedication. I offered to bring her some lunch after we were done, but she declined.

She left to do something in the 'back room' (does anyone really know what goes on back there?) and returned beaming. She told me that I had been such a good customer, she put in a "special" request to get my glasses done by tomorrow morning. I almost fell out of my chair. I had not perceived any change in her attitude up to that point, but I realized that even as she now beamed, her expressions weren't really all that different. She was just one of those people who is hard to read. I left with a whole new appreciation of the power of positive affect and a complementary eyeglass cleaning kit.

As we begin to notice positive traits in others we also begin to notice them in ourselves. As we become less critical of others we become less critical of ourselves. As we shift the mental pattern in how we view others it automatically shifts how we view ourselves. Looking for the good in others is one of the easiest ways to improve our own self-image. It is much easier than trying to deliberately shift negative beliefs about ourselves.

Finding the good or the positive core in ourselves and others will simultaneously awaken and evolve the best of what we can become together. In the next section we look at identifying and leveraging our strengths as a way to further discover our positive core and build positive emotion.

Identifying and Leveraging Strengths

Leadership is about creating an alignment of strengths making people's weaknesses irrelevant. ~Peter Drucker

There are many aspects to our individual positive core, and one is personal strengths. Identifying and leveraging strengths is one way to ignite our positive core and build positive emotion.

Dr. Martin Seligman talks about the factors that lead to a happy and fulfilled life in *Authentic Happiness*. He feels the focus for change should be on building our positive aspects and not on fixing our problem areas, which is consistent with the Positive Principle. Seligman explains:

> I do not believe that you should devote overly much effort to correcting your weaknesses. Rather, I believe that the highest success in living and the deepest emotional satisfaction comes from building and using your signature strengths.[32]

Seligman created a survey that helps determine our signature strengths. He believes that once we know our strengths we can figure out ways to apply them more often. This allows us to be more successful in our endeavors and also experience a higher level of satisfaction. He has an online survey on his website at www.authentichappiness.org. It is called the "VIA Strengths Survey" and takes about 25 minutes to complete. It ranks your strengths and shows how you compare to thousands of other people.

I completed the survey and found the results interesting. I was surprised to learn that forgiveness was my highest strength, but was not surprised that "love of learning" came out at number two and "curiosity/interest in the world" at three. This helps explain why I thoroughly enjoy researching and writing this book. This strength information also helps me decide where best to volunteer my time, and what roles might be a best fit. I know that I will be relatively happy and successful in whatever I choose as long as I am continually learning. It also helps me understand various periods of frustration in my life when learning was not as strong.

Dr. Mel Levine is a children's education expert and pediatrician who is also a proponent of identifying and nurturing strengths. In his book, *A Mind at a Time*, Dr. Levine identifies eight fundamental components of learning, and explains that it is not realistic to expect a child (or adult) to be good at all of them.[33] He states that children have stronger and weaker learning abilities, and yet we expect them to excel in all areas in school.[34] Dr. Lavine begins work with a child by creating a profile of her strong and weak learning components or abilities. He looks at areas where she is strong, and tries to find ways to develop and celebrate her strengths to the fullest. He goes on to identify strategies for helping her cope with areas of weakness or simply avoiding weak areas all together.

Dr. Levine also shows how strengths can be used to overcome weaknesses. He gives numerous examples, such as helping a child who "has trouble learning dates in history but is an excellent artist, so she practices learning dates by making a large illustrated poster with a timeline on it."[35] He also talks about using a child's affinity for a particular subject as a way to help him learn. For example, a child who loves cars can be stimulated to learn by reading and writing about cars.[36]

We can apply these same principles to overcome our weaknesses. The things we like to do also tend to be things we do well, and vice versa. If we have trouble arriving on time to a certain meeting, but love to compete, we might create a game with another late-comer to see who can be on time more often. If we have to bring work home in the evening and love the outdoors, we might take our work on the patio with a favorite drink. If we don't like to cook but love to socialize, we might invite a friend over to prepare meals together for the week ahead. We might listen to books on tape to get us to the gym more often, or listen to favorite music to motivate us to clean.

There are other consultants and experts who agree that building on strengths is more effective than trying to develop weak areas. Peter Drucker writes about it in *Management Challenges for the 21st Century*, and suggests a process called *The Feedback Analysis* to develop strengths.[37] Donald Clifton, who has been called the father of "strengths psychology," and Marcus Buckingham of the Gallup Organization, are also great proponents of focusing on strengths for personal development. They have created a strengths assessment as well, along with books and supporting programs that focus on building strengths as a more effective approach than fixing weaknesses. In addition to providing detailed information about individual strengths, they provide tips for managing others based on their strengths.[38]

There are a variety of ways we can identify and leverage our strengths and interests to enhance our effectiveness and enjoyment. We simply need to know our strengths, and then look for ways to incorporate them in as many areas of our lives as possible. This will bring greater success and enjoyment to our lives than will trying to fix the areas where we are weak. It is also feels a whole lot better.

Final Thoughts

The Positive Principle suggests that personal growth and change are accelerated by focusing on the positive core and other positive aspects of ourselves and situations. Discovering and appreciating what is right builds energy and momentum for change. Identifying and leveraging our personal strengths leads to greater personal effectiveness and fulfillment.

Feeling good is not just a nice fleeting experience, but is essential to optimal functioning and health. It expands our thinking, buffers against depression, and builds resilience in handling future difficulties. It bears testimony to the words of Ralph Waldo Emerson: "Nothing great was ever achieved without enthusiasm."

CHAPTER 6

The Emergent Principles

You cannot step twice into the same river,
for waters are continuously flowing on.

~ HERACLITUS

Appreciative Inquiry (AI) is a living concept that evolves and expands with new knowledge and experience. This is what keeps it alive and relevant and will hopefully prevent it from becoming another "fad." I have added nuances and expanded the original principles a bit to reflect the latest thinking, research, and ideas that have emerged since its inception.

There are five additional principles that have been proposed by AI practitioners to help define the emergent AI concept. The first three were proposed by Diana Whitney and Amanda Trosten-Bloom in 2003 in their book *The Power of Appreciative Inquiry*. They are: The Wholeness Principle, the Enactment Principle, and the Free Choice Principle.[1] These principles were created out of the authors' experience with large-scale organization and community change work. Jackie Stavros and Cheri Torres recommended the Awareness

113

Principle in their 2005 book *Dynamic Relationships: Unleashing the Power of Appreciative Inquiry in Daily Life.*[2] Frank Barrett and Ron Fry are proposing the Narrative Principle in their 2005 book *Appreciative Inquiry: A Positive Approach to Cooperative Capacity Building.*[3] In this chapter we discuss each new principle in turn.

The Wholeness Principle

You must understand the whole of life, not just one little part of it. That is why you must read, that is why you must look at the skies, that is why you must sing, and dance, and write poems, and suffer, and understand, for all that is life. ~Anonymous

"The Wholeness Principle posits that the experience of wholeness brings out the best in people, relationships, communities, and organizations."[4] In the Constructionist Principle we discussed the concept of co-creation and inter-connectedness, and how we are continually influencing and being influenced by those around us. The Wholeness Principle takes this idea one step further and suggests that we are not only influenced by those around us, but are actually part of a bigger collective or whole that is greater than the sum of the individuals.

Our perspective shifts in helpful ways when we are able to experience this sense of wholeness and perceive ourselves within it. We begin to see our role in creating and maintaining the larger communities of which we are a part, and gain greater understanding and compassion for others. We learn to sense the overall patterns and influences that sustain the larger group and become more adept at initiating change. We come to know the symbiotic nature of our relationships, and realize the value of cooperation over competition.

Wholeness versus Reductionism

The concept of wholeness can be contrasted with reductionism or fragmentation. They are ways of perceiving and each has its merits. Fragmentation essentially consists of breaking wholes into discreet parts which can be considered, studied, and worked-with individually. This way of thinking is helpful in such activities as breaking complex tasks into steps, or deciding what each person will do on a work team. Fragmentation can become problematic when we lose sight of the bigger whole and the dynamics that exist between the discreet parts.

The concept of wholeness has been around for centuries. It is reflected in many Eastern and indigenous religions and cultures and is gaining favor in a variety of fields including biology, chemistry, physics, human health, and organizational theory.[5] It is described within such concepts as complex-adaptive systems, dissipative structures, chaos theory, systems thinking, quantum mechanics, complexity science, whole-systems change, and holistic health.

The essential idea of wholeness is one of synergy, where the whole is greater than the sum of the parts. There is an additional layer of complexity in the whole that is lost when it is divided into pieces that are studied separately. Such reductionist or fragmentary thinking is pervasive in Western culture, and physicist David Bohm explains how we have learned to perceive in this way:

> In essence, the process of division is a way of *thinking about things* that is convenient and useful mainly in the domain of practical, technical and functional activities (e.g., to divide up an area of land into different fields where various crops are to be grown). However, when this mode of thought is applied more broadly to man's notion of himself and the whole world in which he lives (i.e., to his self-world view), then man ceases to regard the resulting

> divisions as merely useful or convenient and begins
> to see and experience himself and his world as
> actually constituted of separately existent fragments.
> Being guided by a fragmentary self-world view, man
> then acts in such a way as to try to break himself and
> the world up, so that all seems to correspond to his
> way of thinking.[6]

Bohm is essentially saying that we create the appearance of a
fragmentary world by thinking in a fragmentary way. He states
that fragmentary thinking is deep and pervasive, and has
implications for all aspects of life.[7] It causes us to create
artificial boundaries that create the illusion of separateness. He
believes it is at the heart of our confusion and inability to solve
our social, political, economic, ecological, and psychological
crises.

Bohm suggests we need to give attention to our
fragmentary way of thinking and be aware of it in order to
bring it to an end.[8] Wheatley explains this further:

> The challenge for us is to see past the innumerable
> fragments to the whole, stepping back far enough to
> appreciate how things move and change as a
> coherent entity. We live in a very fuzzy world,
> where boundaries have an elusive nature and seldom
> mean what we expect them to mean. The illusory
> quality of these boundaries will continue to drive us
> crazy as long as we focus on trying to specify them
> in more detail, or to decipher clear lines of cause and
> effect between concepts that we treat as separate, but
> which aren't.[9]

Artificial boundaries block our connection to the whole,
leading us to observe what is going on "out there" in a
detached way. We see ourselves as separate from "them" and
miss the ways we contribute to and sustain the actions of the
whole. For example, we get enraged over a news story about

the destruction of the rain forests, but don't see how we contributed to it with a recent paper towel purchase. We observe increasing violence in our schools and communities, and miss the connection with our own desensitization to violence from watching violent movies. We watch an endearing story of how one family helped another in need, and don't see how our volunteer efforts in a local charity contribute to creating a service-oriented culture.

The point is to recognize that we all have some part in creating the whole we experience. It can be as small as recycling plastic bottles, or as big as organizing a global clean-up campaign. It may be ignoring a situation or escalating one. We each play a role in creating our families, communities, and world, and this realization allows us to be more effective in creating what we want. There is no "they."

Competition versus Cooperation

Competition is an interesting by-product of reductionist thinking. Charles Darwin suggested that species compete for limited resources, and that the strongest survive; however, recent research by Jonathan Weiner suggests that cooperation, and not competition, is the basis of survival. Wheatley and Kellner-Rogers cite Weiner's work conducted on the Galapagos Islands where Darwin first developed the "Survival of the Fittest" notion:

> During good times, one population of cactus-eating finches shared a broad niche: they each ate from many parts of the cactus. But following a drought, birds with beaks only one millimeter longer used this slight extra length to drill into cactus fruits. Their shorter-beaked neighbors focused on fallen cactus pads that they could rip and tear. Scarcity moved them to explore more diversified ways of feeding so that they could continue to live together.

> Similar symbiotic agreements are evident between
> very different species. If bees are absent, certain
> birds will seek flower nectar as part of their diet. If
> bees enter the system, the birds change their dietary
> needs and no longer look to flowers.[10]

We are all part of creating the whole we experience, and a
cooperative model suggests that survival depends on our ability
to work together. We come to realize that what we do as
individuals affects the whole, and vice versa. The illusions of
separateness block our ability to see that when others lose,
some part of us loses as well in the bigger picture. We are
deeply inter-connected as explained in the Constructionist
Principle, a fact which is not always readily apparent in
reductionist thinking.

Being Present to the Emerging Whole

An essential skill in the concept of wholeness is learning to
perceive from this perspective. We are each part of many
bigger organizing schemes such as families, communities,
ecosystems, cultures, and the human species. Our ability to
recognize our connections within these larger webs helps us
understand how they impact us and how we influence them.
This recognition allows us to be more effective in our change
efforts. Wheatley explains:

> The whole must go in pursuit of itself; there is no
> other way to learn who they are. But as people
> engage together to learn more about their collective
> identity, it affects them as individuals in a surprising
> way. They are able to see how their personal patterns
> and behaviors contribute to the whole. The surprise
> is that they then take responsibility for changing
> themselves.[11]

There is a natural flow that emerges in perceiving from the whole, where we move from the whole to thoughts of ourselves, and back to the whole again. The area of greatest inquiry in the wholeness concept is in how exactly to think and act within this new paradigm.

There are a variety of organizational approaches that work with the whole system, such as Open Space Technology, Large-Scale Strategic Change, Future Search, System's Thinking, and AI Summits. These philosophies access the wisdom of the whole by engaging large numbers of people within the system in meaningful activities. For example, it's not unusual to have over a thousand people for two full days of an AI summit, dreaming and designing the future organization together. We can also use these approaches with our families and communities.

There are a variety of spiritual practices that help with this new way of thinking such as meditation and mindfulness. These practices essentially allow one to be more fully present and connected in the moment. If you are new to these concepts and want more information, you might want to try *8 Minute Meditation* by Victor Davich, or *The Miracle of Mindfullness* by Thich Nhat Hanh.

There is a final way to apply the concept of wholeness in our individual lives by simply shifting our attention. We can intentionally choose to observe from this broader perspective and discover a new way of perceiving and experiencing ourselves in relationship with others.

Consider a family dinner. The next time you sit down to eat with your family or a group of friends, try an experiment in perceiving the whole system. Mentally step back and admire the overall flow of conversation and activities. Marvel at the established routines of who sits where, who talks when, what gets talked about, the type of food served, and the unspoken agreements about who does what. Consider all the life experiences this family has shared together and how these experiences have shaped and molded it to what it is today. Pay attention to your feelings and any intuitive thoughts you have about it all.

Now step back further and consider the history of family dinners and what has gone on up to this point. What subtle or not-so-subtle shifts are emerging within the group? For example, do the conversations seem to be more lively recently? Do certain people seem to be doing different things than they have in the past? Remember that whatever we focus on grows, and we can find whatever we want within this experience. Try to look for what you want more of, not less of.

Notice your role in this system. What do you say and do to contribute to the patterns and habits that define this family? Do you like the direction of the subtle shifts you are noticing? In what ways are you supporting the positive shifts? What would happen if you spoke about the shifts you are observing?

Leverage points for change emerge as we effectively sense the bigger picture and our role in creating it. This is a difficult concept to articulate, since this new way of perceiving often requires intuition and feelings in addition to our analytic way of thinking. Wheatley helps explain:

> As I have struggled to understand a system as a system, I have been drawn to move past cognition into the realm of sensation. The German philosopher Martin Heidegger describes this as a "dwelling consciousness." When we dwell with a group or a problem, we move quietly into our senses, away from our sharpened analytic skills. Now I allow myself to pick up impressions, to notice how something feels, to sit with a group or with a report and call upon my intuition. I try to encourage myself and others to look for images, words, patterns that surface as we focus on an issue.[12]

At any moment we can "dwell" in the whole we are part of. We can shift our thinking to pay attention to the larger web of relationships in which we are currently participating. We can move from focusing on our personal experience in a crowded building, to sensing the flow of activity all around us and our part within it. This makes us feel more connected and heightens our ability to understand, work, and live within the systems of which we are a part.

The "whole" is a continually emerging construction, changing in each moment and perceived differently by each person. It requires that we be open in the present to whatever is emerging before us, with as little judgment or expectation as we can muster. Feelings and intuition offer valuable insight into the complexity of whole systems, which cannot be understood through analytic thinking alone.

Reductionist thinking is quite the opposite. Whole systems are considered as relatively fixed entities that we can assess and "box" into logical pieces at any point in time. Intuition and feelings are not particularly important in fragmentary thinking, and may explain their relatively low perceived value in Western culture.

Conclusion

In summary, wholeness offers new ways of comprehending and working within the larger scheme of life. Fragmentation blocks understanding of the whole and creates a perilous illusion of separateness. We lose sight of our role within the system and our ability and responsibility to help move it in the direction we desire. Wholeness creates deeper understandings of the complexity of the system. Ideas for change emerge as we immerse ourselves within the larger community. We can simply shift our thinking to be more continuously aware of the larger web of relationships in which we exist, and awaken to our place within them. We come to realize it is as much about "us" as it is about "me."

The Enactment Principle

Be the change you wish to see in the world.
~Mahatma Gandhi

Whitney and Trosten-Bloom describe the Enactment Principle as, "Positive change comes about as images and visions of a more desired future are enacted in the present."[13] Ralph Waldo Emerson said, "What you do speaks so loud that I cannot hear what you say." This principle is about reflecting on what we do and the degree to which it aligns with what we want. The Enactment Principle suggests that we can create our ideal future by making changes in the present that align with that future.

Embodying What We Want

Robert Fritz uses the term *embodiment* to describe enactment. He writes, "What you embody tends to get created."[14] He explains:

> Those who 'fight for peace' do not embody peace, but rather fighting. Those who worry about their health do not embody health, but rather fear...What you embody speaks louder than your behavior, to the same degree that your actions speak louder than words.[15]

Actions, questions, focus, words, and images all need to align to what we want. Gandhi did not say, "Don't be the change you don't want to see in the world." We might laugh at that, but that's what we do when we focus on getting rid of problems in our lives. Again, I have mentioned this before but it bears repeating. We can only embody what we want to create, and not what we want to eliminate.

The focus of enactment is on activity and not as much on belief. Sometimes it takes a while for our beliefs to catch up with our actions. Changing our actions first is one way to bring our beliefs along with us towards the desired future. It's walking the talk, even when you feel like you're wobbling on your feet.

On a practical level, enactment means practicing new behaviors and actions in the present before we have "reached" our vision. It's an extension of the Anticipatory Principle assumption that big changes begin small. We create big change through our daily incremental conversations and actions that add up to larger changes over time.

The process of enactment is called different things. Fritz refers to it as "create and adjust,"[16] and Senge et al describe it as prototyping:

> In its essence, prototyping accesses and aligns the wisdom of our head, heart, and hands by forcing us to act before we've figured everything out and created a plan...The feedback you get from experiments will give helpful clues about how to shape, mold, and concretize what is beginning to form—but only if you learn to listen and set aside your negative reactions to "not getting it right" from the outset...the result is action shaped by the field of the future rather than by the patterns of the past. [17]

Errors and adjustments are expected and valued in enactment as we learn by trying, correcting, and trying again. In our complex, ever changing, and deeply interconnected world, it is no longer possible to accurately predict what will or won't work. It is only by doing that we discover and create what works in the present.

We learn as we go with enactment, adjusting and shifting our actions based on feedback from gradual implementation. These new behaviors and actions can feel a bit uncomfortable

at first, and feedback is helpful in fine-tuning what will and
will not work. The new actions will begin to feel more
"natural" once they become habituated into our automatic
thinking, which will come from continued practice. Golfer Ben
Hogan claims, "The more I practice the luckier I get."

Experimenting or trying things out is important because
we do not truly know how things will work until we have tried
them. In this sense, our ability to plan is limited. Wheatley and
Kellner-Rogers suggest that it is more important to focus on
what will work during this process rather than on what is
right:[18]

> Many of us have created lives and organizations that
> give very little support for experimentation. We
> believe that answers already exist out there,
> independent of us. We don't need to experiment to
> find what works; we just need to find the answer...
>
> Observing others' successes can show us new
> possibilities, expand our thinking, trigger our
> creativity. But their experience can never provide
> models that will work the same for us. It is good to
> be inquisitive; it is hopeless to believe that they have
> discovered our answers.[19]

Many of us are used to relying on experts for our answers, and
Wheatley and Kellner-Rogers suggest we begin to trust our
own inner wisdom. It is also typically a shift to try things out in
a "half-baked" manner. We are used to neat packages of steps
and sequences that we cleanly and neatly do at the appropriate
times. The messiness and perceived inefficiency of trial and
error can feel very uncomfortable at first. Resources and
experts can still provide valuable help, but the idea is to
incorporate only the relevant aspects and combine or modify
them in conjunction with other ideas.

Just Try It

The trial and error method of learning is the approach children use, and I've become a believer in this approach by watching my 4-year old son. I've watched him work with a ball-tracking game, where you build a structure for a ball to travel through. I have a mechanical engineering degree, and have stood by watching him construct paths that I "know" will not work. I've also read parenting books that say you should let children learn from their mistakes, so I sit and watch him build paths in error, knowing he will ultimately learn by doing.

The first time he constructed something I knew was wrong and it turned out to work, I thought it was a fluke. The second time it happened with a different arrangement, I really began to see how our assumptions of what is right get in the way of finding solutions.

It's like the difference between a fly and a bee in a bottle. Bees are "smarter" than flies, but they have a hard time getting out of open glass bottles. They continue the same strategy of trying to penetrate the glass, and often die before they find a way out. Flies just buzz all around the bottle, banging here and there until ultimately and unintentionally they find their way out the top.

The point is not that flies are better than bees, but that it might be best to try something new when we are stuck, even if it doesn't really make sense. Even though it might not work, we may learn something from the results that leads us to a new understanding. Our attempts are not really as random or meaningless as they might appear. Just try it.

I have to admit I did not see the power of this principle when I first came across it, but I have since become a major supporter. I love to analyze things and am somewhat of a perfectionist. These beliefs and practices have kept me from making change in many areas of my life as I waited for the perfect solution, or the knowledge of exactly what to do and how. Not any more.

I recently read a book called *Positive Discipline*[20] that is consistent with AI principles and encourages family meetings. In the past I never would have gotten around to doing a meeting, since it would have taken an inordinate amount of time to read back through the book and figure out how to do it. I was literally working on the Enactment Principle at the time, and decided to "just try it." I started really small, and our family began by going around the table and saying one good thing about each other. We then briefly discussed chores and that was it. I left out 80% of what was supposed to be in the meeting. It went well.

Each meeting I add one slightly new or different aspect, and it has been one of the best things that has happened in our family. I never would have started these meetings without this principle of "just try it," and it has worked beautifully. I even think that if I had taken the time to learn the "right" way and done it that way from the start, I probably would have scared everyone off, including myself. As we discussed in the Anticipatory Principle chapter, small changes give other people, processes, routines, and structures a chance to change gradually along with us.

Conclusion

Small change becomes big change. We enact the future when we presently act in ways that are consistent with our vision. We can try new behaviors, thinking, and actions that align to our future image to begin embodying the future we desire. This incremental approach lets us learn as we go, adjusting and shifting our behaviors to find what works. When we're really stuck, it's important to remember the fly principle: better to fly like a fly than be like a bee!

The Free Choice Principle

In the truest sense, freedom can not be bestowed;
it must be achieved. ~Franklin D. Roosevelt

The essence of the Free Choice Principle, created by Whitney and Trosten-Bloom, is that "free choice liberates power."[21] "People perform better and are more committed when they have freedom to choose how and what they contribute."[22] It suggests that freedom to act and choose is essential for healthy functioning. Freedom can be supported or restricted by our relationships, institutions, and our own inner thinking. Some believe that shifting our underlying beliefs and assumptions provide the greatest opportunities for personal growth and freedom.

Freedom from Internal and External Forces

There are many different thoughts and theories about freedom. The freedom described in this principle in the context of organizations is freedom from external pressures. It relates to the external influences and forces that keep our organizational decisions and actions in-check. It includes such things as hierarchies, structures, and processes that facilitate or hinder communication, decision-making, and action.

These external forces show up in our personal lives in the relationships and structures in which we live. Freedom to decide and act in certain ways is impacted by agreements we have with other people and institutions. These include such things as fidelity promises with significant others, commitments to care for children and pets, and agreements to abide by the rules and practices of the workplaces, communities and governments of which we are a part. If we fundamentally agree with the qualifiers these relationships and structures put on our choices and actions, then they are not limiting our free choice in the sense described herein.

There are also internal forces that impact our ability to choose freely. Senge describes this in *The Fifth Discipline,* as he cites the wisdom of Bill O'Brien of Hanover Insurance:

> When most people say, "I am free to do what I want," what they mean is: "I have freedom of action. No one is telling me what to do; no one is keeping me from acting as I wish…"

> "People think they are free because of the absence of external controls," says O'Brien. "But in fact, they are prisoners of a deeper and more insidious form of bondage—they only have one way of looking at the world."[23]

Consider a person who feels trapped in a job he dislikes and continues to work there year after year because he truly believes it is the only reasonable way he can provide for his family. In this case there is no one limiting his freedom (though he may try to project the blame onto others.) In actuality, he is captive to his own limiting thoughts about what is possible. Our beliefs can enslave us to an extent just as great as any outside force we may experience. This is why surfacing assumptions is such a powerful activity, as we discussed in the Constructionist and Anticipatory Principle chapters.

The Freedom of Inner Clarity

Margaret Wheatley has another interesting perspective on this internal view of freedom. She suggests that freedom comes from knowing who we are, or what she calls coherence.[24] She talks about this idea within the context of organizations. I see each one of us as, in effect, an organizing system:

> [Coherent Organizations] are free because they know who they are…Coherent organizations experience the world with less threat and more

freedom. They don't create boundaries to defend and preserve themselves. They don't have to keep others out. Clear at their core, they become less and less concerned about where they stop. Inner clarity gives them expansionary range.[25]

I believe the essential idea here, as it relates to the Free Choice Principle, is that clarity about who we are provides the freedom to choose and act wisely and without fear. A clear self-concept creates security about what we do and do not believe, which makes diverse thinking and ideas less threatening. We don't have to worry that contrary ways of perceiving will "sway" us unwillingly or blindly into some dangerous new way of being.

I believe inner clarity is at the heart of diversity issues. If I am not sure enough about who I am, there is a possibility that a different person might unduly influence me. Many people think that valuing diversity is about accepting or being respectful of differences, but this is only the first step. The true value of diversity is realized when we feel safe enough in ourselves to inquire into, appreciate, and learn from the differences in others. In other words, we are able to appreciate the differences in others to the extent we are confident about who we are.

As we become clearer about our self-concept, we begin to release the limiting beliefs we hold, and become more free to pursue our desires. Our self-concept is grounded in certain essential core beliefs and values, and is a continuously shifting construction. When we deliberately reflect on our beliefs and values we become clearer about our identity and have more freedom to exercise choice.

Conclusion

There are many ways to think about freedom, and in this section we considered several perspectives. We can reflect on the choices and actions present in our relationships and institutions, and decide what aspects provide the greatest personal freedom. We can also reflect on our underlying beliefs about our lives and who we are to build greater confidence in exploring differences within others and expanding our potential. We will likely discover that our beliefs hold greater promise for freedom and transformation beyond anything contained in our perceived external constraints. Just remember, whatever we focus on grows. Be sure to inquire into peak moments and experiences of personal freedom to create more of it, and not the ways in which it is lacking in your life.

The Awareness Principle

Let us not look back in anger, nor forward in fear,
but around in awareness. ~James Thurber

The Awareness Principle was proposed by Jackie Stavros and Cheri Torres in their book, *Dynamic Relationships*. It states:

> Full awareness means being self-aware and socially aware. It means understanding yourself in relationship to others, recognizing that dynamic relationships allow options for actions resulting in many possible outcomes for any given situation, and realizing that the outcome desired can be generated by those engaged in community. Full awareness implies that the actions you take are considered and taken with appreciative intent to create positive relationships and vital organizations and communities. Full awareness allows you to recognize the value of reflection and action and the ability to reflect, act, and reflect again with new or beneficial insight that informs your next action.[26]

This principle suggests we become more aware of our automatic thinking habits and intentionally shifting them in ways that are consistent with the AI principles. By continually being open to new ways of positive relating, we can build and sustain healthy relationships. By taking responsibility for our role in the relationships we create, we are more deliberate and intentional in those co-creations. Stavros and Torres propose five ways to practice this principle:

> 1. Know and understand that our relationships are dynamic…
> 2. Reflect in ways that allow us to notice when we are congruent and authentic…
> 3. Attend to the language we use because it influences our relationships and consequently our communities…
> 4. Realize and accept that, as a person living with appreciative intent, we are responsible in all our relationship communities for our role in elevating feelings, processes, and dynamics with others…
> 5. Reflect on emotional reactions in ways that support our ability to stay open, be challenged, and give and receive refusals (saying "no") without losing the appreciative direction…[27]

They suggest that we incorporate the principles of AI into our everyday experiences in many of the same ways we have discussed throughout this book. This includes being mindful of our use of language, questions, focus, and affect with others. We should try to understand how inter-connected we are and the ways we co-create our reality and relationships. They also suggest we continually reflect on our experiences with others to become more aware of the underlying relational dynamics and assumptions. This insight provides clarity, empathy, and ultimately freedom in being able to create more of what we want together.

Reflection basically consists of stopping in the moment of our conversations to consider what is going on in our automatic thinking. Stavros and Torres suggest asking a variety of questions such as, "What is happening or being said? What are the "facts" of the situation and what am I making up? What assumptions am I making? What am I focusing on? How did I immediately perceive what is happening? What questions or actions on my part will move us toward the kind of relationship we want to create together?"[28]

Surfacing Assumptions

A lot of what Stavros and Torres discuss in the act of reflection is surfacing underlying assumptions. David Bohm agrees that our assumptions or opinions are created out of our experiences with others, but he suggests that at some point we begin to identify with our opinions. We become our assumptions and then unconsciously begin to defend them because we are instinctively defending ourselves.[29] He believes this defending is at the heart of our relationship struggles and interferes with creativity.[30] Bohm recommends that we try to *suspend* assumptions in order to learn more about them and how they operate in our relationships:

> …what is called for is to suspend those assumptions, so that you neither carry them out nor suppress them. You don't believe them, nor do you disbelieve them; you don't judge them as good or bad. You simply see what they mean—not only your own, but the other people's as well.[31]

Bohm proposes that the best way to surface assumptions is dialogue, which he describes as a group of people having an open discussion with no purpose, agenda, decisions, conclusions, or leader.[32] Underlying assumptions naturally emerge in these types of conversations, and we can then begin to look at them together consciously. He suggests a few tips for being in these types of conversations, such as noticing your own reactions to what is being said. He explains:

> You have to notice your own reactions of hostility,
> or whatever, and you can see by the way people are
> behaving what their reactions are…And if
> temperatures do rise, those who are not completely
> caught up in their particular opinions should come in
> to defuse the situation a bit so that people could look
> at it. It mustn't go so far that you can't look at it.
> The point is to keep it at a level where the opinions
> come out, but where you can look at them.[33]

The Public Conversations Project[34] out of Boston is doing wonderful work through dialogue. This non-profit organization "promotes constructive conversations and relationships among people who have differing values, world views, and perspectives about diverse public issues." They have convened dialogues to help open understanding between opposing groups on such topics as abortion, the environment, and homosexuality.

The Public Conversations Project dialogues do have facilitators and purpose, but they follow the spirit of dialogue that Bohm suggests. One of their ground rules is, "avoid assigning intentions, beliefs, or motives to others (Ask others questions instead of stating untested assumptions about them.)"[35] We can do this in our daily conversations to build better relationships as Stavros and Torres suggest. Rather than jumping to conclusions about the intent of another, we can ask directly or try and find another construction that is more affirming.

Common Consciousness

There is an even more interesting notion to surfacing assumptions than the obvious improvement in relationships. It is something Bohm calls *common consciousness*. The following excerpts from his work summarize this intriguing idea:

The object of a dialogue...is to listen to everybody's opinions, to suspend them, and to see what all that means. If we can see what all of our opinions mean, then we are sharing a common content, even if we don't agree entirely...

...If everybody sees the meaning together of all the assumptions, then the content of consciousness is essentially the same...

...If we could all share a common meaning, we would be participating together...It would mean that in this participation a common mind would arise, which nonetheless would not exclude the individual. The individual might hold a separate opinion, but that opinion would then be absorbed into the group too. He might or might not keep his opinion, but his meaning would be seen.

Thus, everybody is quite free...there is both a collective mind and an individual mind, and like a stream, the flow moves between them. The opinions, therefore, don't matter so much...we start to move beyond [our opinions] in another direction—a tangential direction—into something new and creative.[36]

Bohm explains how our collective assumptions are generally incoherent, going in all different directions. Our collective thought becomes coherent as we align our thinking by surfacing underlying beliefs. This state of coherent shared meaning is what Bohm is referring to as common consciousness. Defending our underlying assumptions keeps us from reaching this ideal state. He suggests that a group able to operate from a place of common consciousness would be highly effective in creating something new together.

Conclusion

The Awareness Principle suggests that deliberately integrating the principles of AI in our daily lives creates more dynamic and sustainable relationships. We can take responsibility for relating with positive intent, and reflect on our thinking and actions to become more effective at creating what we want together. We can keep our conversations moving in an appreciative direction by learning to surface and suspend our assumptions. We can create more effective and joyful relationships and communities by becoming fully aware of ourselves individually and collectively.

The Narrative Principle

Many a man would rather you heard his story than granted his request. ~Lord Chesterfield

The Narrative Principle, proposed by Frank Barrett and Ron Fry, suggests that "stories weave a connectedness that bridges the past with the future."[37] We create stories about ourselves and our lives that help us organize and make sense of things. Barrett & Fry explain:

> ...coherence, movement and direction are central to 'meaningful' life. Life is not a series of random, unconnected happenings. The past, present and future are not separate unconnected stages, but rather beginnings, middles and endings. . . of a story in progress. We constitute our lives as meaningful by seeing them and expressing them through stories.[38]

Narratives are rich with alternative meanings and positive possibilities. We can transform our lives by shifting our narratives in ways that bring us more of what we want.

How We Create Stories

Stories, or narratives, consist of experiences we have about our lives linked together over time.[39] Therapist Alice Morgan provides a beautiful description of how she might create a story about herself as a good driver in, *What is Narrative Therapy?*

> ...I could string together a number of events that have happened to me whilst driving my car...and interpret them as a demonstration of me being a good driver. I might think about, and select out for the telling of the story, events such as stopping at the traffic lights, giving way to pedestrians, obeying the speed limits, incurring no fines, and keeping a safe distance behind other vehicles.[40]

She goes on to describe how her story gets stronger and richer as she adds more consistent experiences. The stronger her story becomes, the greater her ability to ignore, or edit-out events that don't fit. For example:

> ...the times when I pulled out too quickly from the curb or misjudged the distances when parking my car are not being privileged. They might be seen as insignificant or maybe a fluke in the light of the dominant plot (a story of driving competence). In the retelling of stories, there are always events that are not selected, based upon whether or not they fit with the dominant plots.[41]

Each time Morgan talks about any aspect of herself as a good driver, she tells the story slightly differently. Different people and circumstances cause her to edit out certain parts, or focus on certain aspects over others. For example, if a police officer pulls her over, what she chooses to say and how she frames the story of her driving will be different than when telling her friends later.

The story is not only changing in the re-telling by what she decides to include; she is actually shifting her underlying meaning, beliefs, and assumptions as she co-creates it with each person. We re-author our lives as we tell our stories. As we discussed in the Constructionist Principle, different people and situations will evoke different things from us. The stories we tell become our identity and life experience as Bruner explains:

> Eventually the culturally shaped cognitive and linguistic processes that guide the self-telling of life narratives achieve a power to structure perceptual experience, to organize memory, to segment and purpose-build the very "events" of a life. In the end, we become the autobiographical narratives by which we "tell about" our lives.[42]

Narrative therapists help people re-author their stories in ways that bring them more of what they want. In any given situation there are an endless number of things to focus on and meanings to construct. Narrative therapists help people go back into those rich life experiences and look for helpful *alternative stories* or meanings that were there as well, but were overlooked.[43] These alternative meanings are then woven in or come to replace the dominant story. The essence of personal growth is in changing the negative aspects of our dominant self-image stories into something more empowering or desirable.

Stories are Transformative

Stories are extremely rich in meaning. They are imbued with images, metaphors, values, lessons, and a host of other things that reach deep inside us. Listening to the stories of others can be very powerful. Barrett & Fry explain:

> Because they operate on emotional and metaphoric levels, stories move us before we "know" why we are being moved. They reach us before we have a chance to put up our defenses. Fairy tales retain their power extremities (rich, powerful, ugly, etc.) and serve as potent metaphors for intense wishes and fears. They give a shape to wishes and fears and this is central to their lasting effect.[44]

The stories of others have ways of touching us that leave us forever changed. We can simply listen to the story of another and be transformed. Narrative therapist David Epston keeps a library of success stories and testimonials that he gathers from clients.[45] He claims that simply having a client listen to a powerful story of how another person overcame the same difficulty is sometimes enough to resolve the issue.

The *Chicken Soup for the Soul* books by Jack Canfield and Mark Victor Hansen, et al, contain true endearing stories that have the capacity to transform. I heard a story about a mother who was having trouble getting through to her daughter about the consequences of drinking and driving. A friend gave her daughter the *Chicken Soup for the Teenage Soul* book, and the girl's attitude changed after reading a story about a teenager killed in a drunk driving accident. The story was able to reach the girl in a way the mother could not.

In her book *Annie Stories*, Doris Brett explains how parents can make-up stories for their children to help them work through and overcome their fears.[46] She explains how stories can be helpful in creating a sense of safety by distancing, since it is all happening to someone else. Stories help the child feel understood, and that children are not alone in their problem. Finally, stories provide role models and helpful ideas about what might work. She provides examples of how to create stories that are basically identical to the child's situation, and then tell how the characters resolve the issues.

I did a slightly different version of this when we moved from Ohio to North Carolina. My daughter was four and terrified of the move. She was concerned about a variety of things, but primarily that we would not be able to fit our large kitchen table in the moving truck (go figure). No amount of convincing and looking at moving trucks on the road would change her mind.

I got on the computer and wrote what was really my first book. It was about a 4-year-old girl moving from Ohio to North Carolina, and how the moving truck came and put everything they owned on the truck, including the kitchen table. I included other aspects she was fearful of, along with incredible pictures of the ocean and playgrounds. She was awestruck. I must have read the book a thousand times before we moved, one hundred times after we moved, and I still consider it to be one of my best parenting success stories.

Conclusion

Individuals, couples, families, schools, companies, churches, countries, and cultures all have their stories. These stories contain the local truths of these communities and provide meaning and organization to the life experiences of those who have them. Stories from the past also serve important functions in conveying values, norms, and traditions, which provide continuity and rationale in moving forward.[47] Stories about the future contain powerful images which create that very future, as we discussed in the Anticipatory Principle.

The stories we tell and listen to provide meaning and continuity in our lives. They have transformative power by their very nature and profoundly influence our course. Better stories are those that bring more of what is desired and less of what is not.[48]

Final Thoughts

The five emergent principles round out the AI philosophy. The Wholeness Principle gives voice to the power of relationships, and being present to the continually emerging whole of which we are a part. The Enactment Principle states that we need to embody changes now that we want for the future, and just trying new things is a good place to start. The Free Choice Principle suggests that freedom is found within, and expanding our thoughts and beliefs offers great potential for personal transformation. The Awareness principle reminds us that we are responsible for our role in creating relationships, and following the principles of AI will keep us moving together in an appreciative direction. Finally, the Narrative Principle suggests we create stories to help organize our lives in meaningful ways, and we can transform our lives by re-authoring our stories or simply listening to the stories of others.

And we'll all live happily ever after.

Part II

The Practice

CHAPTER 7

Appreciating-Imagining-Acting Process

We don't have to stay in the same box
we were shipped in.

~ Bill Turner

There is tremendous depth to Appreciative Inquiry (AI,) but we do not have to cognitively understand the principles to live them. It is also possible to understand the theory and not live the principles. I did this myself as an AI consultant for many years. I taught these concepts to others in organizations but did not follow them personally.

Living the principles has transformed my life. It is an ongoing journey of discovery and learning that leads to higher and higher levels of happiness and possibility. I am currently more joyful and fulfilled than I ever thought possible, and I still have much left to learn and incorporate. I'm passionate about sharing what I have found. I love "The Philosophy" part of this book, but the key to changing your life is in "The Practice."

In this chapter we'll explore the Appreciating-Imagining-Acting (AIA) process for incorporating Appreciative Inquiry in our lives. The principles can feel overwhelming, and this process helps apply them in a manageable way. In the next chapter I'll present several exercises to help shift our thinking habits to automatically notice the good and focus on what we want.

Overview of the AIA Process

There is nothing so practical as a good theory.
~Kurt Lewin

The Appreciating-Imagining-Acting (AIA) process is a simple framework to help implement the AI principles in our daily lives. Practicing AI requires conscious, deliberate thinking and action at first. The AIA process provides three basic steps to help with this as shown in the following diagram:

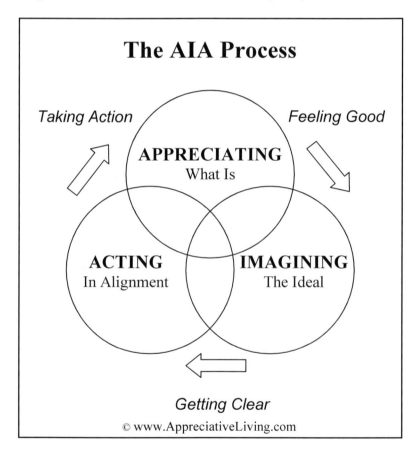

The AIA Process

Taking Action   *Feeling Good*

APPRECIATING
What Is

ACTING   **IMAGINING**
In Alignment   The Ideal

Getting Clear

© www.AppreciativeLiving.com

The steps in the AIA process are: Appreciating what is, Imagining the ideal, and Acting in alignment. The purpose of these steps is to help us feel good about the current situation or person, get clear about what we want, and take action that aligns with our ideal future.

We can think of the AIA process like a set of driving directions. It helps us find an appreciative route from where we are to where we want to go. In the beginning, we need to study the AIA process just as we study a set of directions when traveling somewhere new for the first time. Directions help us get started, stay on course, and arrive at our destination. Each time we travel the route we might try a new road or discover a better way. The AIA process, like a set of directions, provides one of many ways to travel the appreciative journey.

The AIA process keeps us on course by asking three things in our daily interactions and experiences:

1. *Appreciating:* Do I feel appreciative or good about this situation or person? If not, I know I am not focusing on what I want in this situation. How can I shift to see more of the good or more of what I want?

2. *Imagining:* Am I clear about what I want and is this where I'm giving my attention? My feelings again provide helpful information, because if I'm not feeling good, I'm not focusing on what I want.

3. *Acting:* Do my current actions and thinking align with what I want? Is what I'm saying, thinking, and doing consistent with what I desire? If not, what small action can I take that would help move me just a bit closer to my ideal?

I want to reiterate that Appreciative Living is *a journey and not a destination*. It takes time to reconfigure our thinking and behavior habits, and progress can sometimes feel slow. The important thing to remember is that change is always occurring, whether we perceive it or not. We continually move closer to or further from what we want in each moment. The AIA process helps us become more aware of which direction we are moving in, and gives us the tools to live more deliberately and create what we want.

The steps in the AIA process are not always linear. It's easier to think of the steps as orderly and discreet in the beginning, but as you become more familiar with them you will come to understand the overlapping, non-sequential nature. You will take feedback from an action to develop greater clarity about what you want, or to appreciate what's already present. You may enter the process at Step 2 or even 3, and work them in any order. You will begin to experience the overlap as you realize you must feel appreciative in order to create an ideal image, or determine an optimal action. Let's take a deeper look at the three steps in this process.

Appreciating

The first step is appreciating what is. It suggests that we learn to see the good attributes, the available learning, and the positive possibilities of our present experience. Exercises include things like "Gratitude lists," "Finding the Positive Core," "Shifting Focus," and "Reframing." In this step we learn how to appreciate what we have right now.

The essence of Appreciating is to get to a place of feeling good about the present situation or person. We believe from Barbara Fredrickson's work that our cognitive thinking broadens when we feel good, and we are able to generate better solutions and think creatively. We have also discussed that we can only create more of what we want by giving it our attention. If we are not feeling good about a person or situation, we are giving attention to and creating more of what we *do not* want.

Feeling good about "what is" can be accomplished in numerous ways depending on the situation. If we are dealing with a difficult person we might shift by trying earnestly to find some small positive core aspect. If we are facing a stressful situation, we might take an inventory of our strengths and successes, and try to reframe the situation as an opportunity for learning. If we are just feeling bad, we might simply want to go for a walk or do something else that makes us feel better. We can also look through the exercises listed in the Appreciating section in the next chapter and do one that seems to fit.

There is no point in trying to get clear about what we want or to take action when we are angry, sad, or depressed. Acting from these negative places often makes the situation worse. The feeling part of this step is important. Thinking about the good, or finding the good, or seeing the good is the first part of this step. Feeling good is the next level. When we are content, happy, excited, or passionate about something we want, our ability to create it escalates. This is why the first step is to appreciate; to get to a place of positive emotion so we have the cognitive and emotional resources to create positive realities and make wise choices while going forward.

Imagining

The next step is imagining the ideal. On a grand scale, we create an image of what we want most, or what things would look like if they were exactly as we'd have them. We learn to create visions that are so provocative and meaningful, we feel excited and inspired in our everyday lives. On a smaller scale, we decide what we want in the moment. Imagining includes such exercises as "Gaining Clarity," "Envisioning the Ideal," and "Surfacing Assumptions."

The essence of this step is to get clear about what we want. It might be as big as creating a ten-year life vision that encompasses all our hopes and dreams, or as small as mentally acknowledging what we want in a brief conversation. In this step we learn to hold an inspiring image of where we are headed in front of our daily decisions and actions, knowing these images will grow and change along with us.

Feelings are an important part of this step as well. Negative feelings signal we are focusing on what we do not want, and can act as a "stoplight" in helping us realize we need to get clear about what we do want. We often enter the process at this step when we are coming from anger, sadness, or despair. The negative emotion signals us to step-back and get clear about what we want, which is the essence of the imagining step.

Positive emotions are like fuel for our future images. The more exciting and desirable our vision, the more power it has in manifesting. Positive emotions also expand our creative and imaginative repertoires for generating better ideas and loftier images. If we desire an optimal outcome, we must create images from a place of feeling good.

Clear images act like beacons guiding our daily decisions and actions. We will say and do things to preserve the peace if we determine that harmony is our primary objective in a relationship. Knowing we want more fun in our lives will lead us to attend an event we might have previously passed-up. We will ask certain people over if we really want an engaging discussion. Our images and desires guide our actions.

The most difficult part of this step can be choosing what we want. We are so culturally programmed to focus on what we don't like or don't want that it can be difficult to determine what we do want. As with any new skill, we get better at choosing what we want with practice.

Acting

The last step is acting in alignment. This means taking a small step forward to think or behave in ways that are consistent with our greatest future images. The change can (and should) be something small, and does not have to be a physical action. It can be a change in our focus, our questions, or our ways of perceiving. Exercises include "Enacting," "Acknowledging the Good," and "Developing Conversational Awareness."

The essence of this step is to take deliberate action that moves us closer to what we want. This step tends to feel the most comfortable of the three since we are an action-oriented culture in the West. We ideally act in alignment with a greater vision from a place of feeling good, but it doesn't always work this way. Our actions often help clarify what we want, or help us appreciate what we have.

The acting step overlaps with the other two, since appreciating and imagining are both actions. Don't let this confuse you. The essence of this step is making a deliberate choice to do something new, which may in some cases be appreciating what is, or getting clear about the ideal.

All these steps take effort in overcoming our automatic thinking to the contrary. Our new behaviors and thinking may feel contrived or unnatural at first, but they will become more comfortable as we practice and integrate them into our automatic habits. Slower is better with change, since our structures, relationships, processes, and patterns all have to shift with us. The following examples illustrate the use of the AIA process in everyday life.

Practical Examples

Habits are at first cobwebs, and then cables.
~Spanish proverb

Broken Refrigerator

My husband was getting ready to take the children out for the evening so I could work on this book. I was really looking forward to the uninterrupted time and went in the kitchen to say good-by to everyone: And then it happened. I heard this strange creaking sound coming out of the refrigerator. I peaked inside and discovered the milk was luke-warm. I could see my evening was about to change.

In my pre-AI days I would have been really mad. This was not a good time for the fridge to break down. (Is there ever a good time for that?) I was really looking forward to this evening and now I would have to deal with this mess instead. I would previously have spiraled into a heap of negative images and feelings about how we would never find someone to fix this thing tonight, how expensive it would be, all the food that will spoil, and on and on. I spent most of my life thinking like this; but this is not how it happened.

I actually did not experience any negative emotion when I noticed the fridge was broken. My first thought was incredible gratitude that I discovered it had broken before all the food went bad. I still had time to move most of the food into our garage refrigerator, and I began rather happily lugging it out. I considered how the timing of this was pretty good, since we were planning on moving in another year and would need to buy a fridge at that time. This was just a little ahead of schedule, but we could buy it now and move it. You would have to have known me before to realize how drastically different this was. I would have been stomping back-and-forth with anger before, and here I was feeling grateful for a broken refrigerator that invaded my night off.

This is an example of the appreciating step in the process. It's learning to see the good and feel joyful in the midst of a difficult situation. I was not pretending the problem did not exist, or ignoring negative feelings. I was genuinely experiencing positive emotion as I naturally and automatically focused on the good things about this situation. The feelings were not contrived.

The positive emotions and focus do not come naturally at first. It is something we need to practice deliberately in the beginning by using one of the appreciating exercises in the next chapter. Our thinking habits develop over time to do this automatically, and eventually we don't have to stop and intentionally shift from negative to positive thinking. I had always questioned whether it was really possible for a person to shift that dramatically from the negative to the positive, and I can say from experience that it is.

I emptied the fridge and began to think about what we would do. I briefly entertained ideas about what features and colors I would like in a new fridge. I then started thinking about having this one fixed and wondered how I might find someone good. I thought for a few minutes about the traits I really wanted in a repair person; knowledgeable, trustworthy, and available tonight. I was willing to pay a bit more for someone who had all these traits.

This is an example of imagining. I was forming mental pictures of what I wanted. This is also something we have to do deliberately at first, since our automatic thinking tends to form pictures of the problem. I created brief images of the ideal situation and repair person that were grounded in reality. I did not entertain repair horror stories I had heard, and I did not get my heart set on a $10,000 deluxe refrigerator. I could have thought of some of my good repair experiences, but this did not occur to me at the time. I focused on what I wanted in this situation; a service call from a reputable service person who would either fix the fridge or wisely advise us to purchase a new one.

There was another image operating in the background in all this. I have created visions of my ideal life that include stress-free, joyful navigation of daily experiences. This image flashed before me more than once, and I remember being aware of how I was living it. I do believe my ideal life vision was indirectly guiding this experience as well.

I then took the third step and acted in alignment with what I desired. I was clear about what I wanted, so the decision about what to do was obvious. I needed to find a repair person and I knew what kind of person I wanted. I called a few neighbors for references, but that didn't work. I opened the phone book and found someone with a lot of certifications and a guarantee. I just happened to call as the owner was walking out the door, and he agreed to stop by that night on his way home. He turned out to be everything I wanted.

I know that finding this ideal person so quickly may sound like good luck, but it happens to me often now. The universe somehow seems to show up to support me when I am feeling good and clear about what I want. The service man fixed the fridge and the rest is history.

This is a simple example, but broken refrigerators are what most of our lives are about. The "big" moments are few and far between. That night would have been a miserable night for me in the past, and probably would have carried over for several days. I can't honestly say that I handle every situation so well, but it is becoming more the norm than the exception.

Eyeglass Story

This story provides a good example of how we can enter the process anywhere, and move in any direction. In this example I enter at the imagining step, and move backwards through the process. I told this story in the Positive Principle chapter, and now I'll explain how it fits in the AIA process.

I went to buy new eyeglasses and found the woman waiting on me to be rude and inconsiderate. I felt very angry and was not enjoying my purchasing experience. I realized I was feeling negative emotion, which triggered my awareness that I was not following the AI principles.

I realized I was focusing on this woman's negative traits, which were not something I wanted. I then made a conscious choice to apply AI, and entered the process at Step 2 of Imagining. I reflected for a brief moment on what I did want in this situation, and decided it was a pleasant experience and successful outcome.

I knew I could not enjoy my experience while feeling angry towards her, and also knew my outcome depended on her. The better she felt, the better she would perform, and the better the outcome would be. I decided to go to Step 1 of Appreciating, and intentionally look for her good traits. I was able to see that she was competent in her work and a very hard worker. I felt my attitude begin to shift more positively towards her, and decided to move to Step 3 and take action. I told her sincerely what I appreciated about her and this began to shift both of our experiences. In the end I achieved what I wanted by creating a good experience and getting my glasses even sooner than expected.

Final Thoughts

In this chapter I presented the Appreciating-Imagining-Acting (AIA) process for helping us find an appreciative direction, and provided two very different examples. The essence of the process is to remind us of three things:

1. Do I feel good about the present situation or person?

2. Am I clear about what I want?

3. Do my actions and thoughts align with what I want?

If you can answer "yes" to all three questions, you are applying the principles. If the answer is "no," you may want to try one of the exercises in the next chapter.

If you find you are having trouble following the AIA process consistently, take comfort in knowing this is common. You have a lifetime of beliefs and habits to shift, and it will take time. Try to follow the process as best you can, do at least one of the exercises in the next chapter each day, and I promise your life will change. When you do have those frustrating moments when you know you are off track, consider the words of author and coach Stephen Covey: "So what?"[1]

CHAPTER 8

Exercises

We are what we repeatedly do. Excellence, then, is not an act, but a habit.

~ ARISTOTLE

In the previous chapter I explained how the AIA process helps us use Appreciative Inquiry (AI) in our daily interactions. In this chapter I present core exercises that help shift our automatic habits of thought and action to be consistent with the AI principles. These simple exercises embody the concepts of AI, and can be done in as little as 5-15 minutes a day. That's not much to invest in creating the life of your dreams.

The purpose of these exercises is to help you automatically notice more of the good and deliberately create more of what you want in your life. They help you find the silver lining and see the glass "half-full." At first you may not observe much difference, since the changes in your thinking will be slow and gradual. Over time you will begin to notice subtle changes, and will realize that your life seems easier, happier, and more fulfilling.

There is also a learning curve with these exercises. You will have to learn new ways of thinking and perceiving that may at first conflict with current beliefs and habits. For example, it may be difficult to find anything good in a difficult situation. It will get easier the more you practice.

There was a "tipping point" that occurred for me after some period of time in practicing these exercises. I don't know this will be true for others, but there came a time where I noticed that my happiness seemed to begin building at a much greater rate. I suspect it had to do with finally learning how to grow and become stronger from negative experiences rather than just managing or getting through them. This happened as a by-product of learning to see the good. I think it was building the trait that Fredrickson refers to as "resilience." I was not resilient when I first began. My goal was to survive bad experiences at worst, and manage them well at best. Learning to be happy and grow from difficult times seemed to be the turning point for me in really living from a place a joy.

Most of these exercises are deceivingly simple and short. Most can be done in 15 minutes or less, though they may take a bit longer the first few times you do them. The idea is to gradually transform your thinking habits and integrate new ways of being. Slow and steady change is sustainable change. I invite you to just try one of the exercises for a few weeks and see what happens.

Where Do I Begin?

*A journey of a thousand miles must begin with
a single step. ~Lao Tzu*

There are as many ways to begin as there are people reading this, and you can literally do the exercises in any order or frequency that works for you. The exercises are grouped by the three steps of Appreciating, Imagining, and Acting. There are ten exercises altogether.

The exercises were designed to be worked at any level. For example, there is an exercise called "Envisioning the Ideal" where you create an image of your desired future. You can use this exercise to create an image of a wonderful dinner you want to prepare that evening, or to create a complete image of your ideal life. You might spend 5 minutes creating the mental picture, or 55. You can use this exercise daily to create quick ideal images, or yearly to create your personal life vision. The exercises were designed to allow for as much flexibility as possible.

The good news with this design is that you can create a custom solution that works uniquely for you. The tradeoff is that there is not much structure. One way to get started is to simply try each of the ten exercises. There are only ten, and if you do one each day, you will have tried them all in less than two weeks. At that point you will be familiar with the exercises and can find a way to use them that works for you. I typically do about 15 minutes a day of exercises, and rarely more than 30. I have to honestly say there are some days I don't do any. I also meditate/pray for at least 15 minutes each morning, which seems to center me and clear my thinking in ways that are hard to explain. Here are a few suggestions and considerations in getting started.

I would begin with the "Gratitude" exercise #1, and do that every day. It takes less than a minute and can really help shift thinking to notice the positive. When you feel ready to take on more, I would then add one new exercise in addition to gratitude, which can both typically be done in 15 minutes or less. You can rotate through the exercises and do a different one each day to get familiar with each activity. Then I would suggest you simply pick an exercise that you are attracted to each day.

A second approach is to create deliberate, focused change. This is done by staying with the same exercise, category of exercises, or topic for a period of time. For example, if you would really like to shift your thinking to see the good, you may do the appreciating exercises every day for a month or more. If you are dealing with a really difficult problem, you may want to work through each exercise in order, using the problem area as your topic for the exercise.

A third approach is to create periodic practices. For example, you might do an annual personal plan, where you do exercises #1, 2, 6, and 8 from the perspective of your life the previous year and what you want in the next. You could then design regular monthly exercises to help align your thinking and actions to your vision.

A final approach is to simply pick any exercise and get started. The important thing is just to try something. The only way to shift thinking is through experience, and simply reading about the principles is not enough to make change in our lives.

I find that I need to do the practices regularly to keep the appreciative mind-set. Our culture is fairly negative and problem focused, and I realize I'm influenced more easily than I care to admit. I still experience ups and downs, but the ups are longer and higher, and the downs are fewer, shorter, and less painful.

I hope you find these exercises helpful, and if you want a complete program for changing your life for the better, check out my second book on "The Joy of Appreciative Living: Your 28-Day Plan to Greater Happiness Using the Principles of Appreciative Inquiry. I promise that will rock your world for good!

I would love to hear any stories you have about how AI has worked in your life, or thoughts you have about this book. Please visit my website at www.AppreciativeLiving.com or email us at Admin@Apprecativeliving.com I would love to share this journey with you.

Here's to a really great life!...

Summary of Exercises

Appreciating Exercises

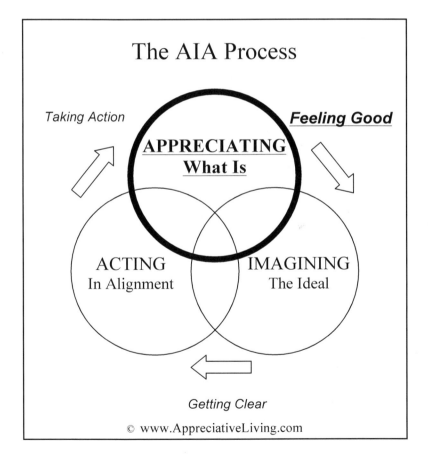

Exercise 1: Gratitude Journal

Primary Purpose: Shift automatic thinking to notice the good
Time: 1-2 minutes a day, every day

Activity: Write at least three things you are grateful for today in a notebook or journal specifically for this purpose. Do this once a day in the morning or evening, and pick something different each time.

Variation: List a person or situation at the top of several pages, and write one daily gratitude for each one. Topics might include your family, your job, specific people in your life, a challenging situation, or your home. This is also a good way to begin slowly shifting your thoughts about a negative person or experience.

Examples: If you are experiencing health problems, keep a page for specifically listing all the positive aspects of your current health. If you want a closer relationship with a co-worker, list him or her at the top of one of your pages.

Considerations: If you find it difficult to list things at first, stay with it. It takes time to shift our automatic habits to notice what is good. I remember days in the beginning where I stretched to come up with things like having enough toothpaste. If you are having trouble listing gratitudes for a difficult relationship or situation, try one of the other exercises first, such as "Reframing" or "Shifting Focus."

Refer to: The Poetic Principle: "Finding What We Want More of, Not Less" (pp. 40-47.) The Positive Principle: "It's Good to Feel Good" (pp. 97-105.)

Exercise 2: Positive Core

Primary Purpose: Find the good in yourself or someone else
Time: 5-10 minutes, daily or as-needed

Activity: Inquire into the positive core of yourself, someone you are close to, or a person in your life with whom you would like a better relationship. List every strength, positive attribute, potential, or good characteristic you can think of. Think of others who like this person (or you) and the qualities you imagine they see. Spend 5-10 minutes writing every positive attribute you can think of. It's important you get to the point of feeling positive emotion or the exercise won't work.

Examples: I did this for my two children, husband, and myself each day for several weeks. I spent 5 minutes on each one of us, and I felt incredible closeness and love during that time. I find that the good thoughts and feelings subside a bit (but they don't disappear) if I don't make time to intentionally focus on them. I also found it was difficult to write about myself at first, but found this to be as important to the success of the process as finding the good in the others.

Variations: Do this exercise mentally when you are with the person. Take a moment to really look for as many good traits as you can find. You don't need to say anything to him or her, but you can if you feel inclined. Notice how you feel as you do this, and if there is a shift in your relationship during this time.

Considerations: If you are doing this exercise with a person you are having a difficult relationship with, and can't get to a place of feeling positive, try doing the "Shifting Focus" or "Reframing" exercises first.

Refer To: The Poetic Principle: "Whatever We Focus On, Grows" (pp. 35-40,) The Positive Principle: "Finding the Positive Core" (pp. 105-109.)

Exercise 3: Reframing

Primary Purpose: Shift perception about a negative situation
Time: 15-20 minutes, as-needed.

Activity: Think about a current difficult situation and try to open yourself to a new perspective or way of perceiving it. Reflect on the following questions and answer the ones that seem relevant:

- How would the following people view my situation—a child, a starving person, a true friend, a homeless person, or someone with a terminal illness?
- How will this issue impact my life ten years from now?
- What is good about this situation, or what can I appreciate?
- What do I really want in this situation? Why?
- What am I focusing on, and how can I shift my focus to notice what I want?
- What do I believe is realistically possible here? How can I expand this belief to broaden the range of possible outcomes?
- What learning is available, and how can I be open to it?
- What one small thing can I do to make this situation just a bit easier or better?

Examples: In the heat of the moment, I believe it is important to honor whatever feelings are showing up – negative or otherwise. In the beginning, I had to deliberately reflect on these questions later, after I "calmed-down." A few of these questions have now become automatic for me, and I will often mentally think through them during a difficult situation. This helps reduce my negative reaction, and helps me think more clearly and productively in the moment.

Variation: Add your own questions to this list. Reflect on the AIA process in chapter 7 and list questions that would help you get back or stay on-track.

Considerations: It is ideally best to begin this exercise from a place of feeling good, but this is not always practical—especially in the heat of the moment. The better you feel when doing this, the better your ideas and insights will be.

Refer to: The Simultaneity Principle (pp. 53-70.)

Exercise 4: Shifting Focus

Primary Purpose: Shift attention to what you want
Time: 20-30 minutes the first day, then 5 minutes daily

Activity: Pick a person or area of your life where you are experiencing difficulty. We grow in the direction of what we persistently ask questions about, and this exercise helps us create more effective questions.

1. List what you don't like or want.
   • I hate doing laundry.
   • Joe is stingy and I don't like going out with him.

2. Determine what it is you really do want in this situation.
   • I want a pleasant laundry experience.
   • I want to enjoy my time out with Joe.

3. Create questions that help you look for and create more of what you want. For example:
   Laundry:
   • What small change can I make today that will make the laundry more pleasant?
   • What do I enjoy or like doing, and is there any way to incorporate some aspect of this into my laundry activity?
   • What strengths do I have that I can leverage in doing the laundry?
   • What best practices are out there for doing laundry?
   Joe
   • What do I enjoy most about going out with Joe?
   • What are Joe's greatest strengths and gifts?
   • What do I appreciate most about Joe?
   • What change can I make, no matter how small, that will help me enjoy my time more with Joe?

4. Pick at least one new question from step 3 to ask each day, or each time the situation arises, and give the answer serious consideration. Your behavior may not change at first, but your thoughts will be shifting. Your behavior should eventually shift in response to your focus on what you want, as long as you sincerely keep asking and answering the new question.

Variation: List the biggest obstacles you believe are in your way of what you want. These are your underlying limiting assumptions. For example, "Laundry is a boring, monotonous task that I have to do every week." Challenge at least one limiting assumption in your new question. For example:

- What could I try with my laundry chore this week that would make it more interesting and enjoyable?
- How can I go more than a week without doing laundry? What if I bought more clothes? What if I did it every day?
- Do I have to do all my laundry? Could someone else do some or all of it? How else could I get clean clothes? Could I barter with someone?

Considerations: You can make this exercise more powerful by doing one of the Imagining exercises along with it. When you decide what you want in step 2, slip in one of the imagining exercises to create your ideal image of what you want. Then go on to step 3 of creating the questions. This will help you create your ideal future image first, and your new questions will become more focused and effective.

Refer to: The Simultaneity Principle: "We Live in the World Our Questions Create" (pp. 54-57,) "Change Begins the Moment We Question" (pp. 57-59,) and "The Unconditional Positive Question" (pp. 59-66.)

Imagining Exercises

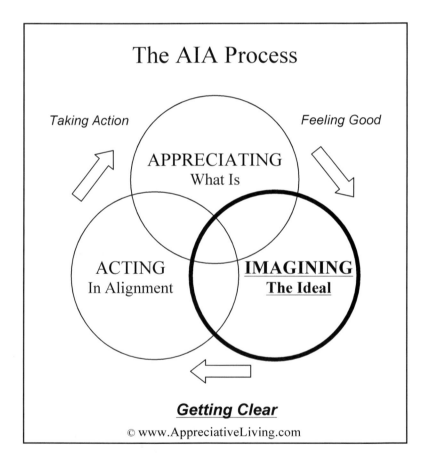

Exercise 5: Gaining Clarity

Primary Purpose: Get clear about what you want
Time: 5-10 minutes, daily (longer if you add the third column)

Activity: Think about your day today and list the major activities on the left side of a piece of paper or computer screen. On the right side, list the 2-3 things you want most from each event. It might be a certain feeling, outcome, learning, or experience. This helps us get clear about what we want, which allows us to be more deliberate in our interactions throughout the day.

Examples: I typically list anywhere from 5-10 major activities on the left, depending on the day. If one activity is driving the children around, I might list on the right that I want to have a pleasant, safe trip and arrive on time. If I am having lunch with a customer, I might list enjoying myself and building a strong relationship.

Variations: Every now and then, go through your day and add a third column listing why you want each thing you do. This is a powerful way to surface assumptions, reduce unhelpful influences from others, and improve your success in creating what you want. It may seem that the reasons are "obvious," but that is the nature of our assumptions. They are assumptions for the simple reason we never question them. For example, I want a pleasant car environment as I drive my children around. Upon further introspection, I realized that what was pleasant for me was not necessarily pleasant for my 4 and 6-year old. Their ideal trip would include laughing and making gross noises the whole way. This realization allowed us to develop a workable solution by including a designated period of "silly time" during the otherwise peaceful ride.

Considerations: This is one of the few exercises that I continue to do everyday. I am now to the point that I often pause before important activities or conversations to reflect momentarily on what I want most out of the exchange. I find it to be one of the most powerful tools in helping me create what I want.

Refer to: The Anticipatory Principle: "Vision Before Decision" (pp. 82-85,) and "We Conceive What We Believe" (pp. 85-89.)

Exercise 6: Envisioning the Ideal

Primary Purpose: Create an ideal future image
Time: 15-30 minutes. Do as needed.

Activity: Select something you want to happen in the future. It might be living the life of your dreams, working in a career you love, or having a wonderful relationship with your teenager.

1. Begin by getting yourself to a place of feeling good in whatever way works for you. It might be listening to music, looking through a photo album, or doing a short version of the positive core exercise. Once you feel good, continue to the next step.

2. Pretend I waved a magic wand, and your ideal _____ (life, career, relationship, etc.) came true in this moment. Write or type every aspect you can think of in this ideal situation. List your thoughts as they stream through your mind, and pretend everything is possible. Let your deepest hopes and desires come forth and dream big about the perfect life, a passionate career, or an incredible relationship with your teenager. Everything is possible. Pretend it is really happening now, and

write in present tense (i.e., "I *am* happy," not "I *will be* happy.") Use the following questions to help guide your thinking.

- What is happening in this ideal situation or relationship?
- How are you feeling?
- What is the best part of all this?
- How does your day go differently now?
- What are you doing that's new?
- Who will be the first to notice and what will they say?

Examples: I do this every so often to create an image of my ideal life. I create a running monologue of every aspect of a wonderful life I can imagine. I often begin by reviewing previous visions to get to a place of feeling good. I start with a blank piece of paper each time and create my vision anew. I find that certain things become more and less important at different times, and I want a vision that reflects what is most important to me right now.

Variations: Create a picture collage of your ideal image. Use magazine cut-outs, clip art, internet pictures, photos, or whatever works to remind you of your ideal. Add key words or phrases. Post it somewhere you can view it regularly.

Considerations: We cannon change other people or external situations, so focus your vision on you and the experience and feelings you most want to experience. We don't need others to change for us to be happy, even though we sometimes believe this. It's a good assumption to investigate. (See Exercise 7)

Refer to: The Anticipatory Principle: "Positive Images Create Positive Futures" (pp. 72-77,) and "The Power of Vision" (pp. 77-81.)

Exercise 7: Surfacing Assumptions

Primary Purpose: Enhance vision and success with change
Time: 10-15 minutes. Do as needed.

Activity: Think about something you really want in your life.

1. Create a brief statement describing what you want. Be sure it is not a statement of what you don't want. For example, use "I want good health" instead of, "I don't want to be sick." Here are some examples:
   • I want a sports car.
   • I want to be physically fit.
   • I want a loving relationship with my mother-in-law.

2. Create a running monologue of why you want this and keep asking why. List every reason you can think of. This exercise will help surface your underlying assumptions about why you desire this, which helps you see where you might need to alter or refine your vision. If you feel you are not getting to a deep enough level as you write, try answering the question "why" at least five consecutive times. For example, "I want a sports car because they are fun to drive. I want to have fun driving because I want to enjoy my life more in general. I want to enjoy my life more in general because I feel like I work all the time. I feel like I work all the time because…"

Example: Here's an example for wanting to be physically fit: I want to be physically fit because research shows I will live longer and have more energy. I want to live longer because I want to be healthy enough to be around and enjoy my grandchildren and great grandchildren. I want to have more energy to really enjoy my life and feel good throughout the day. I want to feel good in my clothes and be able to play golf without being sore the next day. I want to have more energy to get more done at night. If I got more done at night I would have more time in the evening to relax or perhaps take that painting class I've been wanting to take…(keep going)

Variation: You can add a third step to this process by listing all the reasons you believe you will get whatever it is you want. This helps surface deeper assumptions about what you deserve, what is possible, and so forth. Here is an example for wanting to be physically fit: "I will become physically fit because it is important to me, and I am making a solid commitment to myself to do this." (At this point an assumption surfaces that I don't always follow through on my commitments. So, I search within for an honest belief of how I can be successful.) "I am disciplined and follow-through when I have a written plan, so I will create a plan that will insure my success. I was able to keep fit several years ago when…" (Keep going.)

Considerations: This is a powerful exercise for surfacing hidden beliefs or thinking that may be getting in the way of success. It also helps you realize that what you want most when you dig underneath surface material desires, is a positive feeling of love, happiness, excitement, fun, or other positive emotion.

Refer to: The Anticipatory Principle: "Creating Powerful Images (pp. 77-79,) and "Vision Before Decision" (pp. 82-85.) The Free Choice Principle: "The Freedom of Inner Clarity" (pp. 128-129.) The Awareness Principle: "Surfacing Assumptions" (pp. 132-133.)

Acting Exercises

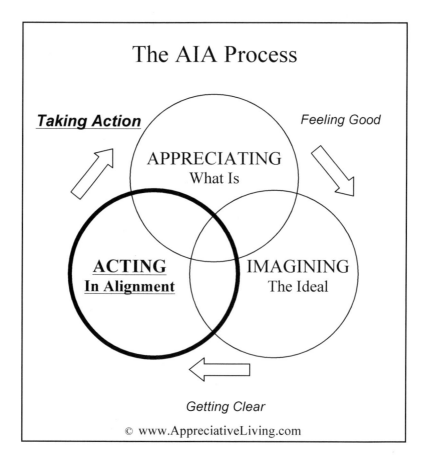

Exercise 8: Enacting

Primary Purpose: Begin making change
Time: 5-10 minutes, daily.

Activity: First create an ideal image of what you want with either the "Envisioning the Ideal" exercise or, "Surfacing Assumptions" exercise. Using that ideal image:

1. Answer this question: "As I step back and reflect on what I really want and where I am today, what do I see as one of the most significant changes I could make that would help me get what I want? What one change would have the greatest impact in helping me achieve what I really desire?"

2. Now ask, "What one small change could I make now, no matter how small, that would align with this high-impact change?" The change does not have to be a physical action, and can be a shift in thinking or attitude.

3. Just try it. Do this one small thing today that will move you in the direction of what you want.

4. Keep doing your small change and modify it if necessary until you find a way it works for you. When the change feels comfortable, or becomes a habit, consider coming back to this exercise and making another small change.

Example: I made a variety of small changes over the last several years in how I care for our home that have had a big impact. Our home is now relatively organized, de-cluttered, and cleaner than ever before. I did this by gradually introducing 15 minute activities suggested by the "FLY Lady," some of which became regular habits. (Visit her free website at www.flylady.net.)

Variation: Consider doing this exercise with a friend. Discuss ways to support each other in making the change and sticking with it. You don't need to work on the same thing, but you can if you like.

Considerations: If you find you are having trouble making the new change or sticking with it, try doing the "Shifting Focus" exercise with your area of difficulty.

Refer to: The Anticipatory Principle: "Big Change Begins Small" (pp. 89-95.) The Enactment Principle (pp. 122-126.)

Exercise 9: Acknowledging the Good

Primary Purpose: Build positive feelings in a relationship
Time: 5-10 minutes, as-needed.

Activity: Make a point to tell someone today what you appreciate about him. The compliment must be sincere, and will have the greatest effect if it is specific. For example, it is better to tell John you appreciate the level of detail he provided in his last report, rather than telling him he did a good job. If appropriate, give the compliment in front of others, but be sensitive to any possibility of embarrassment.

Examples: This exercise can be as simple as telling your friend that you appreciate the way she calls to check on you, or telling the receptionist that he handled your call very professionally. It can be as extensive as thanking your parents for specific ways they have helped you throughout your life, or telling your child what you love most about her in great depth. Again, the compliment must be sincere and should be specific.

Variations: You can write a letter instead of telling the person, or leave a little note on the mirror, desk, or other place where the person will see it. This can be an especially powerful exercise to help a difficult relationship.

Considerations: This is a nice follow-up activity to the gratitude journal. We come to really appreciate others as we do a gratitude list on them, and it adds to the positive momentum in our relationship when we tell them.

Refer to: The Constructionist Principle: "We are Deeply Inter-Connected" (pp. 22-26.) The Poetic Principle: "Tracking and Fanning" (pp. 42-46.) The Wholeness Principle (pp. 114-121.)

Exercise 10: Developing Conversational Awareness

Primary Purpose: Become more intentional in conversations
Time: 10-15 minutes, do anytime.

Activity: Select a conversation you will be having today with another person.

1. Be aware during that conversation of the following:
   - Try to be aware of how you are a creating a new reality with this other person as you both speak. You could talk about anything, and your choice about what to discuss, what it means, and whether it is good or bad is all being subjectively decided in the moment. You are creating your experience of reality together.
   - Make a point to reflect when you feel positive emotion during the conversation:
     o Notice what you are talking or thinking about during those times.
     o Notice what the other person is saying or doing
     o Notice the words or metaphors being used.
     o Study every aspect of this part of the conversation to try and understand what facilitates positive constructions.
   - Pay attention to your discussions about future events and notice the images you build in your mind. Realize that you are creating the future as you speak.

2. Take a few minutes after the conversation to reflect:
   - What was the reality you created together? What other realities were also possible?
   - What kind of future realities did you create? Do you see the similarity in what you think and say about the future and the actual future you experience?

- What were the factors that contributed to positive constructions in your conversation? What kinds of things did you talk about that felt good? How can you do more of that in future conversations?
- How have you changed from this conversation? There is now something different about what you believe or think, or something has been reinforced. Notice how conversations change us in some way.

Examples: This exercise really hit me hard when I first did it. I happened to try it with a friend who was going on about her cousin, and I became brutally aware of my role in helping her sustain and even build this negative construction. I thought I was being supportive in the past by being a good listener, but realized I was instead moving her into a more negative experience with her cousin by giving it even more attention.

Variations: Try this exercise with your internal dialogue. We are continually having conversations with ourselves and bringing in the voices of others. Spend a few minutes thinking about something you have coming up, or a situation you are experiencing. Pause and reflect on your internal thinking and answer the same questions above for your internal dialogue. Pay special attention to the words you use with yourself.

Considerations: This is an advanced exercise, but learning to be more deliberate in conversations is one of the most powerful tools available for creating what we want in our lives. I would suggest reading the sections referred to below to really be able to understand and do this exercise.

Refer To: The Constructionist Principle: "Reality is Co-Created" (pp. 11-14.) The Anticipatory Principle: "We Conceive What We Believe" (pp. 85-89.) The Awareness Principle (pp. 130-135.) The Narrative Principle (pp. 135-139.)

CHAPTER 9

Appreciative Living Summary

Good things, when short, are twice as good.

~ Gracian

Please visit www.AppreciativeLiving.com if you are interested in sharing any of the material in this chapter with others.

Definitions

What Is Appreciative Inquiry (AI)?
- A positive, strength-based approach to change
- Finding the best in people and the world around them
- Co-creating inspiring future images
- Focusing on what we want more of
- Finding and unleashing the positive core
- To learn more: www.appreciativeinquiry.cwru.edu

What Is Appreciative Living?
- Applying the principles of AI in daily life
- To learn more: www.AppreciativeLiving.com

The Five Original Principles of AI

The Constructionist Principle
- Reality and Identity are Co-created
    - There is no one reality or identity, but multiple perceptions
    - Reality and identity are co-created in relationship with others
    - Reality and identity are continuously changing
    - Reality and identity are a collective group of opinions from which different people and situations evoke different things
- Truth is Local[1]
    - There is no absolute truth
    - Local truths exist as agreements within communities of people who hold similar beliefs
    - Local truths are extremely important
- We See Things as We Are
    - There are no neutral observers
    - We filter experience through our beliefs
    - Most of our beliefs were unconsciously adopted
    - It's critical to reflect on our beliefs
- We Are Deeply Interconnected
    - We are continually influencing and being influenced by others
    - What others think about us strongly affects us and vice versa
    - Some suggest we exist within a deeper underlying connecting field
- Words Create Worlds
    - Reality is constructed through language
    - Language is inadequate to fully convey meaning
    - Metaphors don't just describe a thing, they create it
    - Word choice is important

To learn more visit: www.AppreciativeLiving.com   ©2005 J.Kelm

The Poetic Principle

- Life Experience is Rich
  - o Each moment and person contains infinite possibilities for interpretation
  - o Each moment and person has many untapped positive accounts
- We Have Habits of Seeing
  - o We tend to notice the same things over and over
  - o What we notice is driven by our co-created beliefs and assumptions
- Whatever We Focus On, Grows
  - o Whatever we pay attention to becomes a bigger part of our experience
  - o If we focus on problems, we create more problems. If we focus on success, we create more success[2]
  - o Focusing consecutively on positive or negative thoughts creates a corresponding positive or negative spiral
- Finding What We Want More of, Not Less of
  - o We can only create more of something, not less
  - o If we are against something or don't want it, we are indirectly creating more of it with our attention
  - o For example, we cannot create "no more war" or "no more financial struggle"
  - o We can create peace and financial abundance
- Developing an Appreciate Eye
  - o Affirming describes the positive aspects of what we see
  - o Appreciating goes beyond affirming, by generating new ways of seeing
  - o Appreciating is achieved by inquiring deeply into positive aspects
  - o What we find to be positive, pleasant, beautiful, etc. is socially influenced

The Simultaneity Principle

- We Live in the World Our Questions Create
  - We continually ask questions internally and externally
  - Questions direct our attention and action
  - All questions are leading questions[3]
- Change Begins the Moment We Question
  - Change begins in the moment we ask or answer a question
  - Initial questions frame our experience going forward
  - There are no neutral questions
- The Unconditional Positive Question
  - Unconditional positive questions are generative and transformative
  - Unconditional positive questions:
    - Ask about positive experiences, strengths, successes, hopes, images
    - Are grounded by referring to peak experiences and best practices
    - Challenge limiting beliefs and assumptions in positive ways
    - Generate new insights and ways of knowing
- Living in Wonder
  - A spirit of wonder naturally generates positive questions
  - Wonder is facilitated by openness and curiosity
  - Wonder is at the heart of appreciative inquiry

The Anticipatory Principle

- Positive Images Create Positive Futures
  - Our images or visions of the future create that very future
  - Images are more powerful creators than abstract ideas or plans

- o Images are continuously provided in our culture, families, etc.
- The Power of Vision
    - o Positive future images precede the rise of cultures and negative images precede the fall[4]
    - o The most powerful images have cognitive, emotional, aesthetic, and spiritual components[5]
- Vision Before Decision
    - o Powerful visions provide clarity in decision-making and action
    - o Conscious choices are those made in alignment with future images[6]
    - o We automatically take on images of culture, family etc. unless we deliberately choose otherwise
- What We Believe, We Conceive
    - o Future images are created from our beliefs and assumptions
    - o Our beliefs about what's possible are some of the most limiting
- Big Change Begins Small
    - o Change is continuous and often imperceptible
    - o Small incremental changes lead to large sustainable change

The Positive Principle

- It's Good to Feel Good
    - o Positive emotions [7]
        - ▪ Broaden thinking and range of actions
        - ▪ Undo lingering negative emotions
        - ▪ Fuel psychological resiliency
        - ▪ Fuel upward spirals towards improved emotional well-being
    - o Successful marriages have a 5:1 ratio of positive to negative moments[8]

- o Happy people are healthier, more productive, live longer, and perform better than unhappy people[9]
- The Positive Core
    - o All people, organizations, and experiences have a positive core
    - o The positive core consists of such things as strengths, achievements, opportunities, wisdom, unexplored potentials, and assets
    - o The positive core expands as it is affirmed and appreciated
- Identifying and Leveraging Strengths
    - o Building strengths is more effective than correcting weaknesses
    - o Strengths can be leveraged to help in weaker areas

The Five Emergent Principles of AI

The Wholeness Principle[10]

- Wholeness Versus Reductionism
    - o We are part of a bigger "whole" or interconnected web of relationships
    - o The whole cannot be understood by studying individual parts (fragmentation)
    - o Fragmented or reductionist thinking is culturally pervasive
    - o Fragmented thinking breeds competition instead of cooperation[11]
- Being Present to the Emerging Whole
    - o To experience the whole, we need to use intuition and feelings in addition to cognition
    - o Awareness of the whole awakens us to our role in creating and sustaining it

The Enactment Principle[12]
- Embodying What We Want
  - Be the change you wish to see
  - If we "fight for peace" we embody fighting, not peace[13]
- Just Try It
  - Just try a new behavior that aligns with what you want
  - Start small and gradually introduce new behaviors
  - Expect errors and adjustments as you experiment

The Free Choice Principle[14]
- Freedom from Internal and External Forces
  - Institutions and relational agreements impact freedom to choose and act
  - Beliefs and assumptions are often the greatest inhibitors of freedom
- The Freedom of Inner Clarity[15]
  - Clarity of who we are provides security and confidence to pursue life freely
  - Inner clarity comes from reflecting on underlying beliefs and assumptions

The Awareness Principle[16]
- Social and Self Awareness
  - Awareness is understanding and integrating the AI principles
  - We are responsible for our role in co-creating positive sustainable relationships
  - We need to use cycles of action and reflection, where we act, reflect, and act with awareness[17]
- Surfacing Assumptions
  - Reflecting on our automatic thinking is important
  - Surfacing and suspending assumptions is key in good relationships

To learn more visit: www.AppreciativeLiving.com   ©2005 J.Kelm

The Narrative Principle[18]

- We Construct Stories About Our Lives
    - Stories are formed by linking experiences over time
    - We preference some events over others in creating our stories, or narratives
    - We can change our stories to help bring us more of what we want
- Stories are Transformative
    - Stories are rich with meaning, images, metaphors, values, and lessons
    - Stories reach us before we can put up our defenses[19]
    - Listening to the stories of others can be transformative

The Appreciating-Imaging-Acting (AIA) Process

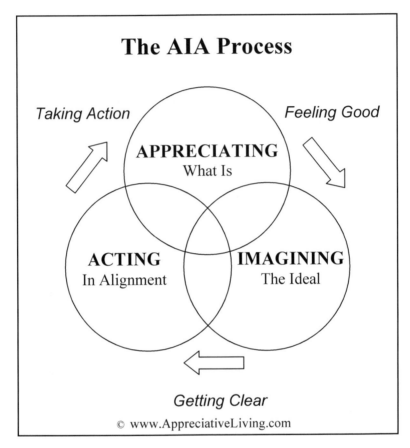

Appreciating
- Finding what's right with the situation or person
- Ask: Do I feel good about this person or situation?

Imagining
- Creating inspiring images of the ideal future
- Ask: Am I clear about what I want?

Acting
- Taking small steps to move forward
- Ask: Do my thoughts and actions align with my wants?

To learn more visit: www.AppreciativeLiving.com   ©2005 J.Kelm

Summary of Exercises

Appreciating

Exercise 1: Gratitude Journal
   Shift automatic thinking to notice the good.
Exercise 2: Positive Core
   Find the good in yourself or someone else.
Exercise 3: Reframing
   Shift perception of a negative situation.
Exercise 4: Changing Focus
   Shift attention to what you want.

Imagining

Exercise 5: Gaining Clarity
   Get clear about what you want.
Exercise 6: Envisioning the Ideal
   Create an ideal future image.
Exercise 7: Surfacing Assumptions
   Enhance vision and success with change.

Acting

Exercise 8: Enacting
   Begin making change.
Exercise 9: Acknowledging the Good
   Build positive feelings in a relationship.
Exercise 10: Developing Conversational Awareness
   Become more intentional in conversations.

To learn more visit: www.AppreciativeLiving.com   ©2005 J.Kelm

EPILOGUE

A Proposition….

Diving deep into the principles of Appreciative Inquiry has been an amazing professional and personal exploration. I have been thinking about, talking about, researching, and writing about the principles for almost two years. The book has emerged into something quite different than how it first began. My learning was exponential and the writing and rewriting was extensive. I feel I am finally beginning to get a sense of the whole of AI.

I realize now that this book came out of an implicit question I had: "What does it mean to apply AI in personal life?" As I look at the principles, I am in awe of the breadth and depth of the answers. Some concepts are broad and deep like those in the Constructionist Principle, and some are narrow like those in the Simultaneity Principle. Some are more conceptual, like those in the Anticipatory Principle, while some are more practical, like in the Enactment Principle. There are also overlaps in some of the concepts, such as those in the Constructionist and Positive Principles that tend to underlie the other principles.

As I sit back and reflect on the magnitude of concepts represented, I realize I'm intrigued now with a new set of questions. What might happen if we were to repackage the principles in a way that was more clear, concise, consistent, and complete? How would AI be advanced by a set of principles that were more easily grasped?

I think a simpler, more "user-friendly" version of the principles could propel AI into a whole new domain. I'm not talking about simplifying or re-wording the existing principles, but taking all the principles together as a whole and creating something new. A new metaphor? A new image? What about a new set of 3-5 principles that more clearly and concisely encompasses all the concepts? It is exciting to think of the ways AI could be furthered by making the principles more accessible to all.

There is one additional construct I would include in this new package. I would describe it in current terminology as "The Self-Organizing Principle." It would include relevant concepts from chaos theories and living systems theories on such things as emergent structures, instability and chaos, equilibrium, boundaries, and evolvement into higher orders. It would essentially describe the new thinking around how we change, evolve, grow and organize as living systems.

Perhaps repackaging of the principles could be a topic for the next significant AI gathering. Perhaps it will be the topic of my next book. I had better tell my husband to get ready to eat more hot dogs while I get to work.

END NOTES

Introduction

[1] Cooperrider and Srivastva, *Appreciative Inquiry in Organizational Life.*
[2] Watkins and Mohr, *Appreciative Inquiry,* 15.
[3] Cooperrider and Whitney, *A Positive Revolution in Change,* 3.
[4] Ibid., 14-17.
[5] Whitney and Trosten-Bloom,*The Power of Appreciative Inquiry,* 55.
[6] Barrett and Fry, *Appreciative Inquiry.*
[7] Stavros and Torres, *Dynamic Relationships.*

Chapter 1: The Constructionist Principle

[1] Cooperrider and Whitney, *A Positive Revolution in Change,* 14-15.
[2] Anderson, *Conversation, Language, and Possibilities,* xvii.
[3] Ibid., 5.
[4] Walter and Peller, *Recreating Brief Therapy,* 27.
[5] Seiling, "Moving from Individual to Constructive Accountability."
[6] Ban Breathnach, *Simple Abundance*, Aug. 1.
[7] Gergen, *An Invitation to Social Construction*, 35-57.
[8] Gergen and Gergen, *Social Construction,* 19.
[9] Ibid., *Social Construction,* 20.
[10] Covey, *The Seven Habits of Highly Effective People*, 237-260.
[11] Henricks, *Conscious Living,* 39.
[12] Senge, *The Fifth Discipline*, 80.
[13] Ibid., *The Fifth Discipline*, 80.
[14] Cooperrider, "Positive Image, Positive Action," 100.
[15] Ibid., 100-101.
[16] Ibid., 100.
[17] Reprinted with permission of the publisher. Wheatley, M. *Leadership and the New Science,* ©1999 by M. J. Wheatley, Berrett-Koehler Publishers, Inc., San Fransisco, CA. All rights reserved.www.bkconnection.com p. 20.
[18] Bohm, *Wholeness and the Implicate Order.*
[19] Sheldrake, *Seven Experiments That Could Change the World: A Do-it Yourself Guide to Revolutionary Science.* NY: Riverhead.
[20] Jung, *Archetypes and the Collective Unconscious.*

[21] Reprinted with permission of the publisher. Wheatley, M. *Leadership and the New Science,* ©1999 by M. J. Wheatley, Berrett-Koehler Publishers, Inc., San Franscisco, CA. All rights reserved.www.bkconnection.com p. 53.

[22] Senge, et al, *Presence,* 201.

[23] Ibid., 201.

[24] Senge, et al, *Presence,* 247-253. They mention that Emoto's method builds on earlier work of Dr. Lee H. Lorezen. M. Emoto (1999) *Messages from Water.* (Tokyo: IHM General Research Institute, pg 139.) Also see www.hado.net.

[25] Senge, et al, *Presence,* 250.

[26] Ibid., 250-251.

[27] Reprinted with permission of the publisher. Wheatley, M. *Leadership and the New Science,* ©1999 by M. J. Wheatley, Berrett-Koehler Publishers, Inc., San Franscisco, CA. All rights reserved.www.bkconnection.com p. 35.

[28] Stavros and Torres, *Dynamic Relationships,* 43.

[29] White and Epston, *Narrative Means to Therapeutic Ends*, 28-30.

[30] Gergen, *An Invitation to Social Construction,* 19-30, 47.

[31] Weick, *Sensemaking in Organizations*, 4.

[32] Gergen, *An Invitation to Social Construction*, 65.

[33] O'Hanlon and Weiner-Davis, *In Search of Solutions,* 68.

[34] Ibid., 68.

[35] Ibid., 73.

[36] Reprinted with permission of the publisher. Wheatley, M. J. and Kellner-Rogers, M. *A Simpler Way,* ©1999 by Wheatley & Kellner-Rogers, Berrett-Koehler Publishers, Inc., San Francisco, CA. All rights reserved. www.bkconnection.com p. 38.

[37] Seiling, *The Membership Organization,* 73.

[38] Walter and Peller, *Recreating Brief Therapy,* 38.

Chapter 2: The Poetic Principle

[1] Cooperrider and Whitney, *A Positive Revolution in Change,* 16.

[2] White and Epston, *Narrative Means to Therapeutic Ends.*

[3] Cooperrider and Whitney, *A Positive Revolution in Change,* 3.

[4] Teresa, *Mother Teresa: In my Own Words*, 21.

[5] Senge, et al, *Presence*, 28.

[6] Seligman, *Authentic Happiness,* 95-97.

[7] Cooperrider and Whitney, *A Positive Revolution in Change,* 7.

[8] Odell, "Women's Empowerment."

[9] Reprinted with permission of the publisher. Wheatley, M. *Leadership and the New Science,* ©1999 by M. J. Wheatley, Berrett-Koehler Publishers, Inc., San Francisco, CA. All rights reserved.www.bkconnection.com p. 65.

[10] Reprinted with permission of the publisher. Wheatley, M. *Leadership and the New Science,* ©1999 by M. J. Wheatley, Berrett-Koehler Publishers, Inc., San Franscisco, CA. All rights reserved.www.bkconnection.com p. 65.

[11] Zukav, *The Dancing Wu Li Masters,* 79.

[12] Walter and Peller, *Recreating Brief Therapy,* 75.

[13] Ibid., 75.

[14] Reprinted with permission of the publisher. Wheatley, M. J. *Leadership and the New Science,* ©1999 by M. Wheatley, Berrett-Koehler Publishers, Inc., San Franscisco, CA. All rights reserved.www.bkconnection.com p. 37.

[15] Cooperrider and Whitney, *A Positive Revolution in Change,* 3.

[16] Walter and Peller, *Recreating Brief Therapy,* 74.

[17] Ibid., 75.

[18] Modified and reproduced by special permission of the Publisher, Davies-Black Publishing a division of CPP, Inc., Mountain View, CA 94043 from *Clear Leadership* by Gervase R. Bushe. Copyright 2001 by Davies-Black Publishing. All rights reserved. Further reproduction is prohibited without the Publisher's written consent, pp. 166-178.

[19] Modified and reproduced by special permission of the Publisher, Davies-Black Publishing a division of CPP, Inc., Mountain View, CA 94043 from *Clear Leadership* by Gervase R. Bushe. Copyright 2001 by Davies-Black Publishing. All rights reserved. Further reproduction is prohibited without the Publisher's written consent, p.166.

[20] Modified and reproduced by special permission of the Publisher, Davies-Black Publishing a division of CPP, Inc., Mountain View, CA 94043 from *Clear Leadership* by Gervase R. Bushe. Copyright 2001 by Davies-Black Publishing. All rights reserved. Further reproduction is prohibited without the Publisher's written consent, p. 167.

[21] Modified and reproduced by special permission of the Publisher, Davies-Black Publishing a division of CPP, Inc., Mountain View, CA 94043 from *Clear Leadership* by Gervase R. Bushe. Copyright 2001 by Davies-Black Publishing. All rights reserved. Further reproduction is prohibited without the Publisher's written consent, p. 170.

[22] Ford, *The Right Questions,* 100-101.

[23] Ibid., 103.

[24] Seligman, "Happiness Interventions that Work."

[25] Ibid.,

[26] Cooperrider, "Positive Image, Positive Action," 122.

[27] Ibid., 121-124.

[28] Simmons, *How to Be the Life of the Podium,* 104.

[29] Bohm, *On Creativity,* 6.
[30] Cooperrider, "Positive Image, Positive Action," 121.
[31] Kaufman, *Happiness is a Choice,* 131.
[32] Kiser, "Flying" www.inspirationalstories.com Taken July, 2005.

Chapter 3: The Simultaneity Principle

[1] Cooperrider and Whitney, *A Positive Revolution in Change*, 15.
[2] Ibid., 1.
[3] Adams, *Change your questions, change your life.*
[4] Whitney, et al, *Encyclopedia of Positive Questions,* ix.
[5] Adams, *Change your questions, change your life,* 26.
[6] Walter and Peller, *Recreating Brief Therapy,* 9.
[7] Cooperrider and Whitney, *A Positive Revolution in Change*, 4.
[8] Ibid., 16.
[9] Owen, *The Power of Spirit,* 74.
[10] Whitney and Trosten-Bloom, *The Power of Appreciative Inquiry,* 59.
[11] Senge, et al, *Presence,* 207.
[12] Cooperrider and Whitney, *A Positive Revolution in Change*, 16.
[13] Whitney, et al, *Encylcopedia of Positive Questions,* 65.
[14] Cooperrider and Whitney, *A Positive Revolution in Change,* 17-28.
[15] Bushe and Coetzer, "Appreciative Inquiry as a Team-Development Intervention," 13.
[16] Cooperrider, "Positive Image, Positive Action," 104.
[17] Ibid., 119.
[18] Ibid., 119.
[19] Whitney, et al, *Encylcopedia of Positive Questions.*
[20] The AI listserve is hosted by the University of Utah, and the list manager is Jack Brittain. For subscription information go to: http://mailman.business.utah.edu:8080/mailman/listinfo/ailist
[21] Cooperrider, AI Listserve posting. (2001).
[22] Cooperrider, "The 'Child' as Agent of Inquiry."
[23] Ibid., 10.
[24] Ban Breathnach, *Simple Abundance.*
[25] Hoyt, *Some Stories are Better than Others*, 4.
[26] Anderson, *Conversation, Language, and Possibilities,* 60.
[27] Walter and Peller, *Recreating Brief Therapy,* 36-37, 61.
[28] Ibid.
[29] Csikszentmihalyi, *Flow,* 348-350.
[30] Cooperrider and Srivastva, *Appreciative Inquiry in Organizational Life*, 163.

Chapter 4: The Anticipatory Principle

[1] Cooperrider and Whitney, *A Positive Revolution in Change*, 17.
[2] Senge, *The Fifth Discipline,* 166.
[3] Nicklaus and Bowden, *Golf My Way,* 79.
[4] Fritz, *The Path of Least Resistance,* 123.
[5] Cooperrider, "Positive Image, Positive Action," 110-111.
[6] O'Hanlon and Weiner-Davis, *In Search of Solutions*, 17.
[7] Ibid., 24.
[8] Ibid., 109.
[9] Ibid., 102.
[10] Fritz, *The Path of Least Resistance,* 122-123.
[11] Ibid., 123-124.
[12] Cooperrider, "Positive Image, Positive Action," 114.
[13] Senge, *The Fifth Discipline*, 206.
[14] Cooperrider, "Positive Image, Positive Action," 113.
[15] Ibid., 111.
[16] Ibid., 111.
[17] Senge, et al, *Presence,* 138.
[18] Cooperrider and Whitney, *A Positive Revolution in Change*, 5.
[19] Ibid., 6.
[20] Fritz, *The Path of Least Resistance,* 117.
[21] Reprinted with permission of the publisher. Wheatley, M. J. *Leadership and the New Science,* ©1999 by M. Wheatley, Berrett-Koehler Publishers, Inc., San Franscisco, CA. All rights reserved.www.bkconnection.com p. 55-56.
[22] Cooperrider, "Positive Image, Positive Action," 119.
[23] Ford, *The Right Questions,* 23.
[24] Ibid., 22.
[25] Ibid., 7.
[26] Covey, *The Seven Habits of Highly Effective People.*, 97-144.
[27] Fritz, *The Path of Least Resistance,* 163-166.
[28] Ibid., 164.
[29] Ibid., 165.
[30] Ibid., 164.
[31] Cooperrider, "Positive Image, Positive Action," 119.
[32] Ibid., 119.
[33] *New Webster's Dictionary and Thesaurus.*
[34] Kaufman, *Happiness is a Choice,* 39.
[35] Senge, *The Fifth Discipline,* 81.

[36] Reprinted with permission of the publisher. Wheatley, M. J. *Leadership and the New Science,* ©1999 by M. Wheatley, Berrett-Koehler Publishers, Inc., San Franscisco, CA. All rights reserved.www.bkconnection.com p. 78.

[37] O'Hanlon and Weiner-Davis, *In Search of Solutions,* 42.

[38] Cooperrider, "The 'Child' as Agent of Inquiry," 10.

[39] Cilley, *Sink Reflections.*

[40] www.flylady.net

[41] O'Hanlon and Weiner-Davis, *In Search of Solutions,* 41.

[42] Senge, *The Fifth Discipline,* 63.

[43] Reprinted with permission of the publisher. Wheatley, M. J. and Kellner-Rogers, M. *A Simpler Way,* ©1999 by Wheatley & Kellner-Rogers, Berrett-Koehler Publishers, Inc., San Franscisco, CA. All rights reserved. www.bkconnection.com p. 70.

[44] Reprinted with permission of the publisher. Wheatley, M. J. *Leadership and the New Science,* ©1999 by M. Wheatley, Berrett-Koehler Publishers, Inc., San Franscisco, CA. All rights reserved. www.bkconnection.com p. 132.

[45] Reprinted with permission of the publisher. Wheatley, M. J. and Kellner-Rogers, M. *A Simpler Way,* ©1999 by Wheatley & Kellner-Rogers, Berrett-Koehler Publishers, Inc., San Franscisco, CA. All rights reserved. www.bkconnection.com p. 73.

Chapter 5: The Positive Principle

[1] Cooperrider and Whitney, *A Positive Revolution in Change,* 17.

[2] Taken from title: Fredrickson, "The Value of Positive Emotions."

[3] Fredrickson, "The Role of Positive emotions…," 219.

[4] Frederickson and Branigan, "Positive emotions broaden…," 315.

[5] Ibid., 315-316.

[6] Fredrickson, "Positive emotions and upward spirals…," 172.

[7] Fredrickson, "Positive emotions broaden…," 315.

[8] Fredrickson and Johnson, "'We all look the same to me'…," 5.

[9] Ibid., 14.

[10] Fredrickson and Levenson, "Positive Emotions Speed Recovery…."

[11] Fredrickson, "Cultivating positive emotions…"

[12] Fredrickson, "The Role of Positive emotions…," 222-223.

[13] Fredrickson, et al, "What good are positive emotions in crisis?" 373.

[14] Ibid., 374.

[15] Kaufman, *Happiness is a Choice.*

[16] Fredrickson, "The Role of Positive emotions…," 223.

[17] Ibid., 223.

[18] Fredrickson, "Positive emotions and upward spirals...," 169.

[19] Fredrickson, et al, "What good are positive emotions in crisis?" 373.

[20] Fredrickson, "Positive emotions and upward spirals...," 171.

[21] Ibid., 172.

[22] Cousins, *Anatomy of an Illness,* 27.

[23] Ibid., 39.

[24] From website article, www.RxLaughter.org/message.htm taken in May, 2005

[25] Rath and Clifton, *"How Full is Your Bucket?"* 55.

[26] Gottman, *Why Marriages Succeed or Fail.*

[27] Seligman, *Authentic Happiness,* 40-41.

[28] Taken from title: Fredrickson, "The Value of Positive Emotions."

[29] Whitney and Trosten-Bloom, *The Power of Appreciative Inquiry,* 67.

[30] Cooperrider and Whitney, "A Positive Revolution in Change," 3.

[31] Whitney and Trosten-Bloom, *The Power of Appreciative Inquiry,* 68.

[32] Seligman, *Authentic Happiness,* 13.

[33] Lavine, *A Mind at a Time,* 23, 30.

[34] Ibid., 23.

[35] Ibid., 283.

[36] Ibid., 284

[37] Drucker, *Management Challenges for the 21st Century,* 163-168.

[38] Buckingham and Clifton, *NOW, Discover Your Strengths,* 148.

Chapter 6: The Emergent Principles

[1] Whitney and Trosten-Bloom, *The Power of Appreciative Inquiry,* 55.

[2] Stavros and Torres, *Dynamic Relationships.*

[3] Barrett and Fry, *Appreciative Inquiry.*

[4] Whitney and Trosten-Bloom, *The Power of Appreciative Inquiry,* 69.

[5] Wheatley, *Leadership and the New Science,* 10-13.

[6] Bohm, *Wholeness and the Implicate Order,* 3.

[7] Ibid., 20.

[8] Ibid., 9.

[9] Reprinted with permission of the publisher. Wheatley, M. J. *Leadership and the New Science,* ©1999 by M. Wheatley, Berrett-Koehler Publishers, Inc., San Franscisco, CA. All rights reserved.www.bkconnection.com p. 43.

[10] Reprinted with permission of the publisher. Wheatley, M. J. and Kellner-Rogers, M. *A Simpler Way,* ©1999 by Wheatley & Kellner-Rogers, Berrett-Koehler Publishers, Inc., San Franscisco, CA. All rights reserved. www.bkconnection.com p. 43.

[11] Reprinted with permission of the publisher. Wheatley, M. J. *Leadership and the New Science,* ©1999 by M. Wheatley, Berrett-Koehler Publishers, Inc., San Franscisco, CA. All rights reserved. www.bkconnection.com p. 144.

[12] Ibid., 141.

[13] Whitney and Trosten-Bloom, *The Power of Appreciative Inquiry,* 72.

[14] Fritz, *The Path of Least Resistance,* 208.

[15] Ibid., 208, 210.

[16] Fritz, *Your Life as Art.*

[17] Senge, et al, *Presence,* 151-152.

[18] Reprinted with permission of the publisher. Wheatley, M. J. and Kellner-Rogers, M. *A Simpler Way,* ©1999 by Wheatley & Kellner-Rogers, Berrett-Koehler Publishers, Inc., San Franscisco, CA. All rights reserved. www.bkconnection.com p. 22.

[19] Ibid., 21.

[20] Nelsen, *Positive Discipline.*

[21] Whitney and Trosten-Bloom, *The Power of Appreciative Inquiry,* 75.

[22] Ibid., 55.

[23] Senge, *The Fifth Discipline,* 285-286.

[24] Reprinted with permission of the publisher. Wheatley, M. J. and Kellner-Rogers, M. *A Simpler Way,* ©1999 by Wheatley & Kellner-Rogers, Berrett-Koehler Publishers, Inc., San Franscisco, CA. All rights reserved. www.bkconnection.com p. 60.

[25] Ibid., 60.

[26] Stavros and Torres, *Dynamic Relationships,* 79.

[27] Ibid., 83.

[28] Ibid., 100-101.

[29] Bohm, "On Dialogue," 4, 21.

[30] Ibid., 15.

[31] Ibid., 12.

[32] Ibid.

[33] Ibid., 13.

[34] Public Conversations Project website is www.PublicConversations.org

[35] Public Conversations Project Online article. *Sample Ground Rules (Agreements) for Dialogue.* (1999). Taken July, 2005. www.publicconversations.org/pcp/uploadDocs/SampleGroundrules.pdf

[36] Bohm, *"On Dialogue,"* 15.

[37] Barrett and Fry, *Appreciative Inquiry.*

[38] Ibid.

[39] White and Epston, *Narrative Means to Therapeutic Ends,* 79.

[40] Morgan, *What is Narrative Therapy?*

[41] Ibid.

[42] White and Epston, *Narrative Means to Therapeutic Ends,* 127.
[43] Ibid., 15.
[44] Barrett and Fry, *Appreciative Inquiry.*
[45] White and Epston, *Narrative Means to Therapeutic Ends,* 164.
[46] Brett, *Annie Stories,* 10-12.
[47] Barrett and Fry, *Appreciative Inquiry.*
[48] Hoyt, *Some Stories are Better than Others,* 17, 22.

Chapter 7: Appreciating-Imagining-Acting Process

[1] Covey, *The Seven Habits of Highly Effective Families,* 9.

Chapter 9: Appreciative Living Summary

[1] Gergen and Gergen, *Social Construction,* 20.
[2] Odell, "Women's Empowerment."
[3] Hoyt, *Some Stories are Better Than Others,* 144.
[4] Cooperrider, *"Positive Image, Positive Action,"* 111.
[5] Ibid., 111.
[6] Ford, *The Right Questions,* 22.
[7] Fredrickson, "The role of positive emotions."
[8] Gottman, *Why Marriages Succeed or Fail.*
[9] Seligman, *Authentic Happiness,* 40-41.
[10] Whitney and Trosten-Bloom, *The Power of Appreciative Inquiry,* 69-71.
[11] Reprinted with permission of the publisher. Wheatley, M. J. and Kellner-Rogers, M. *A Simpler Way,* ©1999 by Wheatley & Kellner-Rogers, Berrett-Koehler Publishers, Inc., San Franssico, CA. All rights reserved. www.bkconnection.com p. 43.
[12] Whitney and Trosten-Bloom, *The Power of Appreciative Inquiry,* 72-74.
[13] Fritz, *The Path of Least Resistance,* 208, 210.
[14] Whitney and Trosten-Bloom, *The Power of Appreciative Inquiry,* 75-79.
[15] Reprinted with permission of the publisher. Wheatley, M. J. and Kellner-Rogers, M. *A Simpler Way,* ©1999 by Wheatley & Kellner-Rogers, Berrett-Koehler Publishers, Inc., San Franssico, CA. All rights reserved. www.bkconnection.com p. 60.
[16] Stavros and Torres, *Dynamic Relationships,* 79-83.
[17] Ibid.
[18] Barrett and Fry, *Appreciative Inquiry.*
[19] Ibid.

BIBLIOGRAPHY

Adams, Marilee G. *Change your questions, change your life*. San Francisco, CA: Berrett-Koehler, 2004.

Anderson, Harlene. *Conversation, Language, and Possibilities*. New York: BasicBooks, 1997.

Barrett, Frank & Fry, Ron. *Appreciative Inquiry: A Positive Approach to Cooperative Capacity Building*. Chagrin Falls, OH: Taos Institute Publishing, 2005.

Bohm, David. *Wholeness and the Implicate Order*. London, England: Routledge, 1980.

Bohm, David. *On Dialogue*, Edited transcription of meeting that took place November 6, 1989 in Ojai California following a seminar given by Bohm. Edited by David Bohm.

Bohm, David. *On Creativity*. London, England: Routledge, 1998.

Ban Breathnach, Sarah. *Simple Abundance*. New York: Warner Books, 1995.

Brett, Doris. *Annie Stories*. New York: Workman Publishing, 1988.

Buckingham, M. & Clifton, D, O. *NOW, Discover Your Strengths*. New York: The Free Press, 2001.

Bushe, Gervase R. *Clear Leadership*. Palo Alto, CA: Davies-Black Publishing, 2001.

Bushe, G. & Coetzer, G. "Appreciative Inquiry as a Team-Development Intervention: A Controlled Experiment." *Journal of Applied Behavioral Science 31* (March 1995).

Cilley, Marla. *Sink Reflections*. New York: Bantam, 2002.

Cooperrider, David. "The 'Child' as Agent of Inquiry" *Appreciative Inquiry: An Emerging Direction for Organization Development.* Champaign, IL: Stipes Publishing, 2001.

Cooperrider, D.L, & Srivastva, S. *Appreciative Inquiry in Organizational Life*. Research in Organization Change and Development. Vol. 1. Edited by W. Pasmore and R. Woodman. JAI Press, 1987. This article can also be found at the AI Commons website at www.appreciativeinquiry.org.

Cooperrider, D. L. "Positive Image, Positive Action: The Affirmative Basis of Organizing," *Appreciative Management and Leadership*. San Francisco, CA: Jossey-Bass, 1990.

Cooperrider, D.L, & Whitney, D. *A Positive Revolution in Change: Appreciative Inquiry*. Taos, NM: Corporation for Positive Change, 1999. This article can also be found at the AI Commons website at www.appreciativeinquiry.org. It was also reprinted in, Cooperrider, D. Whitney D., & Stavros, J. *Appreciative Inquiry Handbook.* Bedford Heights, OH: Lakeshore Publishers, 2003.

Cousins, Norman. *Anatomy of an Illness: As Perceived by the Patient.* New York: Bantam Books, 1979.

Covey, Stephen, R. *The Seven Habits of Highly Effective Families*. New York: Golden Books, 1997.

Covey, Stephen, R. *The Seven Habits of Highly Effective People*. New York: Simon and Schuster, 1989.

Csikszentmihalyi, Mihaly. *Flow*. New York: HarperCollins, 1996.

Davish, Victor. *8 Minute Meditation*. New York: Berkley, 2004.

Drucker, Peter, F. *Management Challenges for the 21st Century*. New York: HarperCollins, 1999.

Ford, Debbie. *The Right Questions*. New York: Harper Collins, 2004.

Fredrickson, Barbara, L. "Cultivating Positive Emotions to Optimize Health and Well-Being." *Prevention and Treatment*, Vol. 3, article 0001a, (2000).

Fredrickson, Barbara, L. "Positive emotions and upward spirals in organizational settings." In, Cameron, K., Dutton, J. & Quinn, R. *Positive Organizational Scholarship*. San Francisco, CA: Berrett-Koehler, 2003.

Fredrickson, Barbara, L. "The Role of Positive Emotions in Positive Psychology." *American Psychologist,* Vol. 56, No. 3, (2001).

Fredrickson, Barbara, L., "The Value of Positive Emotions: The emerging science of positive psychology is coming to understand why it's good to feel good," *American Scientist*, 91, 330, (2003).

Fredrickson, Barbara, L. "What Good Are Positive Emotions?" *Review of General Psychology*, 2, 300-319, (1998).

Frederickson, B. L., & Branigan, C. "Positive Emotions Broaden the Scope of Attention and Thought-Action Repertoires," *Cognition and Emotion.* 19 (3), (2005).

Fredrickson B. L., & Johnson, K.J, ""We all look the same to me:' Positive emotions eliminate the own-race bias in face recognition." *Psychological Science.* In-press. (2005).

Fredrickson, B. L., & Levenson, R. W. "Positive Emotions Speed Recovery from the Cardiovascular Sequelae of Negative Emotions." *Cognition and Emotion*, 12, (2), (1998).

Fredrickson, B. L., Tugade, M. M., Waugh, C. E., & Larkin, G. R. "What Good are Positive Emotions in Crisis? A Prospective Study of Resilience and Emotions Following the Terrorist Attacks of the US On September 11, 2001." *Journal of Personality and Social Psychology*, Vol. 84, No. 2, (2003).

Fritz, Robert. *The Path of Least Resistance*. New York: Ballantine Books, 1989.

Fritz, Robert. *Your Life as Art*. Newfane, VT: Newfane Press, 2002.

Gergen, Kenneth. J. *An Invitation to Social Construction*. Thousand Oaks, CA, London: SAGE, 1999.

Gergen, K.J., & Gergen, M. *Social Construction: Entering the Dialogue*. Chagrin Falls, OH: Taos Institute Publishing, 2004.

Gottman, John. *Why Marriages Succeed or Fail: And How You Can Make Yours Last.* New York: Simon & Schuster, 1995.

Henricks, Gay. *Conscious Living: Finding Joy in the Real World.* San Francisco, CA: Harper, 2001.

Hoyt, Michael. *Some Stories are Better than Others.* Philadelphia, PA: Bruner/Mazel, 2000.

Jung, Carl, G. *Archetypes and the Collective Unconscious. (Collected works of C.G. Jung, Vol. 9, Part I)* Bollingen, 1981.

Kaufman, Barry. *Happiness is a Choice.* New York: Random House, 1991.

Lavine, Mel, M.D. *A Mind at a Time.* New York: Simon & Schuster, 2002.

Morgan, Alice. *What is Narrative Therapy? An Easy to Read Introduction.* Adelaide, South Australia: Dulwich Centre, 2000.

New Webster's Dictionary and Thesaurus. Danbury, CT: Lexicon Publications, Inc., 1993.

Nhat Hanh, Thich. *The Miracle of Mindfulness: A Manual on Meditation.* Boston, MA: Beacon Press, 1976.

Nicklaus, J. & Bowden, K. *Golf My Way.* New York: Simon & Schuster, 2005.

Nelsen, Jane. *Positive Discipline.* New York: Random House, 1981.

Odell, Malcolm. J. *Women's Empowerment: The Role of Appreciative Planning and Action in Women's Empowerment/WORTH.* Taken from the AI Commons website from AI Written Works: Stories from the Field. (Mar 2004). at: http://ai.cwru.edu/practice/bibAiStoriesDetail.cfm?coid=6220

O'Hanlon, W. & Weiner-Davis, M. *In Search of Solutions.* New York: Norton & Company, 2003.

Owen, Harrison. *The Power of Spirit.* San Francisco, CA: Berrett-Koehler, 2000.

Rath, T. & Clifton, D. O. *How Full is Your Bucket?* New York: GALLUP PRESS, 2004.

Seiling, Jane, G. "Moving from Individual to Constructive Accountability." Unpublished dissertation, University of Tilburg, The Netherlands, 2005.

Seiling, Jane, G. *The Membership Organization: Achieving Top Performance in the New Workplace Community.* Palo Alto, CA: Davies-Black, 1997.

Seligman, Martin E. P. *Authentic Happiness.* New York: Simon & Schuster, 2002.

Seligman, Martin E.P., "Happiness Interventions that Work: The first results." *AHC Newsletter* Vol. 2 No. 10, (2004).

Senge, P. M., Scharmer, C. O., Jaworski, J. Flowers, B. S. *Presence.* Cambridge, MA: SoL, 2004.

Senge, Peter, M. *The Fifth Discipline.* New York: Doubleday, 1990.

Simmons, Sylvia. *How to Be the Life of the Podium: Openers, Closers & Everything In Between to Keep Them Listening.* New York: AMACOM, 1991.

Stavros, J. & Torres, C. *Dynamic Relationships: Unleashing the Power of Appreciative Inquiry in Daily Living.* Chagrin Falls, OH: Taos Institute Publishing, 2005.

Teresa, Mother. *Mother Teresa: In My Own Words.* New York: Gramercy Books, 1996.

Walter, J.L., & Peller, J.E. *Recreating Brief Therapy.* New York: WW. Norton & Company, 2000.

Watkins, J. M. & Mohr, B. J. *Appreciative Inquiry: Change at the Speed of Imagination.* San Francisco, CA: Jossey-Bass/Pfeiffer, 2001.

Weick, Karl. *Sensemaking in Organizations.* Thousand Oaks, CA: Sage Publications, 1995.

Wheatley, Margaret J. *Leadership and the New Science*. San Francisco, CA: Berrett-Koehler, 1999.

Wheatley, M.J., & Kellner-Rogers, M. *A Simpler Way*. San Francisco, CA: Berrett-Koehler, 1999.

White, M. & Epston, D. *Narrative Means to Therapeutic Ends*. Adelaide, South Australia: Dulwich Centre, 1990.

Whitney, D., Cooperrider, D., Trosten-Bloom, A., Kaplin, S. *Encylcopedia of Positive Questions*. Vol 1. Euclid, OH: Lakeshore Publications, 2002.

Whitney, D. & Trosten-Bloom, A. *The Power of Appreciative Inquiry*. San Francisco, CA: Berrett-Koehler, 2003.

Zukav, Gary. *The Dancing Wu Li Masters: An Overview of the New Physics*. New York: Bantam, 1980.

INDEX

Constructionist Principle, 9-30, 181

Conversations
awareness, 58, 119-120, 130-132, 178; constructing reality in, 10-12, 178; creating future images, 86-90; openness, 68-69; Public Conversations Project, 133; surfacing assumptions, 132-133

Cooperrider, David
Anticipatory Principle, 71, 73, 78, 82; appreciative eye, 47; beginnings of AI, 3-4; Constructionist Principle, 9; positive core, 105; Simultaneity Principle, 53, 57, 58, 62, 66-69; topic choice, 37

Covey, Stephen
Fifth habit, 21; Second habit, 83; 155

Csikszentmihalyi, Mihaly, 69

creativity, 47-48

curiosity, developing, 69-70, *see also* wonder

Darwin, Charles, survival of the fittest, 117

decisions or choices, clarity around, 83-85, 184; conscious, 82-83

depression, 46, 92, 101

dialogue *see* conversations

diversity, 21, 129

Drucker, Peter, 111

Emoto, Masaru, freezing water research, 24-25

enacting or embodying, 122-126, 175, 186

Enactment Principle, 122-126, 140, 186

Encyclopedia of Positive Questions (Whitney, Cooperrider, Trosten-Bloom and Kaplin), 54, 59, 63

Epston, David, 26, 138

exercises
how to begin, 157-159; purpose, 156-157; summary of, 160, 189; appreciating, 161-167; imagining, 168-173; acting, 174-179

eyeglass story, 107-108, 154-155

feelings or emotions
as guidance system 39-40, 147-150; adding power to images, 77-78; intuitive, 118-121; positive, 97-105; of wonder, 67-68

flamingo example, 41, 64

FLY lady, Marla Cilley, 92, 175

focus or attention
experience is rich 31-33; habits, 33-35; focus is fateful, 35-39; finding what we want more of, 39-49, 64, 66, 74, 107, 182; on the whole, 119-121;

Ford, Debbie, *The Right Questions*, 45-46, 82-83

fragmentation, 115-117, 121, 185

Fredrickson, Barbara, 97-103, 148, 157,

Free Choice Principle, 4, 113, 127-130, 140, 186

freedom
from other forces, 127-128, 186; of inner clarity, 128-130, 186

ABOUT THE AUTHOR

I am not only here to be, I am also here to become.
~Goethe

As I write this last page, I realize my life finally makes sense. I look back on my seemingly disparate experiences and see how each played a part in where I am today. I have found my passion and my calling in this work. I have finally found joy.

My undergraduate degree was a BS in mechanical engineering, but I was always fascinated with individual and group dynamics. I received an MBA from Case Western Reserve University with a concentration in organization behavior, where I was introduced to Appreciative Inquiry in a class taught by David Cooperrider. I was immediately enamored with the idea, and was able to apply it as a manager in the Leadership and Organization Change group for a large consulting firm.

I left the corporate world in 1999 to be home with my children, and began an earnest quest to use AI in my daily affairs. My life began to transform as I applied the principles, and I experienced happiness and joy beyond anything I believed was possible for me. I became passionate about sharing it with others and this first book was born.

Several years later I did a wildly successful national joy study using appreciative exercises that led to my second book: *The Joy of Appreciative Living: Your 28-Day Plan to Greater Happiness through the Principles of Appreciative Inquiry.*

In 2013 when I thought I had it all figured out, I experienced medication-induced anhedonia (a type of depression) that took me into deep despair for almost a year. I was able to pull myself out with Appreciative Living, and am more of a believer than ever in the power of this work.

While my life is not perfect, I live with greater joy than I ever dreamed. And my greatest hope is that you will too.

To learn more about Appreciative Living
including workshops, coaching, and more
please visit us at:

www.AppreciativeLiving.com

or email:
Admin@AppreciativeLiving.com

Made in the USA
Middletown, DE
23 January 2020